Common Good

Common Good

Reflections on Everyday Vices and Virtues

Dean Abbott

WIPF & STOCK · Eugene, Oregon

COMMON GOOD
Reflections on Everyday Vices and Virtues

Copyright © 2021 Dean Abbott. All rights reserved. Except for brief quotations in critical publications or reviews, no part of this book may be reproduced in any manner without prior written permission from the publisher. Write: Permissions, Wipf and Stock Publishers, 199 W. 8th Ave., Suite 3, Eugene, OR 97401.

Wipf & Stock
An Imprint of Wipf and Stock Publishers
199 W. 8th Ave., Suite 3
Eugene, OR 97401

www.wipfandstock.com

PAPERBACK ISBN: 978-1-7252-5914-0
HARDCOVER ISBN: 978-1-7252-5915-7
EBOOK ISBN: 978-1-7252-5916-4

09/27/21

For Mr. Willis, who got me started.

Contents

Acknowledgments | ix

1. An Introduction to Vice and Virtue | 1
2. Understanding Vice | 9
3. Self-Indulgence | 16
4. Frivolousness | 23
5. Sloth | 32
6. Unforgiveness | 41
7. Covetousness | 50
8. Fearfulness | 59
9. Gossip | 68
10. Resentment | 77
11. Understanding Virtue | 87
12. Discipline | 96
13. Sober-Mindedness | 105
14. Frugality | 114
15. Friendliness | 123
16. Domesticity | 132
17. Curiosity | 141
18. Non-Attachment | 151
19. Love | 161
20. Virtue and Happiness | 170

Bibliography | 179

Acknowledgments

MANY PEOPLE CONTRIBUTED TO the development of this book. A few deserve special mention. I would like to thank John Pepple for lending me his editorial help and philosophical expertise, the staff of the Fredericktown Community Library in Fredericktown, Ohio for their unflagging support and encouragement, and my parents, Gerald and Faye Abbott for a lifetime of love and for teaching me my first lessons in virtue.

1

An Introduction to Vice and Virtue

A Moment of Clarity

I RECALL WITH VIVID clarity hating a man I had never met. I think his name was Dan. My hatred for him was short-lived. I did not have the self-discipline required to hate him long-term. That would have been too much work. Rather, I hated him for just a few minutes while he sat, literally, in the spotlight.

He had been invited to play piano in a college convocation while we were both students. He played superbly what sounded to my untrained ears like a very difficult piece. When he finished, everyone applauded.

I don't remember whether I applauded or not. What I do remember are the feelings of envy and shame that swept through me. I was looking at a man my age on stage being applauded by our classmates for his superlative achievement in music. To top it off, someone announced that Dan was not a music major, but a pre-med major who had just been accepted into a prestigious medical school. The musical skill we had all just witnessed was not the result of a focused, full-time endeavor, but the result of spare time well spent.

I could do nothing as well as this guy played piano. If he had developed his musical skills to that level of proficiency in just his spare time, I felt I must be doing something wrong. Looking back, it's clear that I was. Instead of pursuing my studies wholeheartedly the way getting into a top medical school requires, I plugged along, achieving far less than I could have, distracting myself with socializing, television, and worry. My college career, rather than being marked by the wise use of time, was characterized by aimlessness and purposelessness.

In the end, the difference between me and Dan was a difference of virtue and vice. Dan had cultivated virtues I had neglected. The hours I had spent in pointless amusement, he had spent learning the structures of music and of the human body. Such choices naturally involved a level of self-denial I had never undertaken, a level of focus I had never achieved. The sum of our choices put us each in our respective places that day, me in the back of a crowded auditorium looking for some way to justify my resentment and him on stage being applauded by every cute girl we knew.

This is not to say that Dan was a good person and I was a bad one. It's not that simple. I wasn't a bad person. I cared about my friends, was curious about the world, hungered for depth, and took moral and philosophical issues seriously. For all I know, behind the scenes, Dan could have been an embezzler, a sadist, or just an ordinary jerk. To say that his achievement and my lack of it was a matter of virtue and vice is neither a simple moral endorsement nor a criticism. Human beings are complicated creatures. Our moral and spiritual growth doesn't happen equally in every area of life simultaneously. It is entirely possible to be a person who, for example, possesses a great deal of self-discipline and who yet lacks compassion, or a person who possesses intense empathy, and yet lacks wisdom.

The Moral Nature of Life

Such human complexity necessitates thinking deeply and clearly about both virtue and vice. By committing to a more precise examination of moral matters, we spare ourselves and others difficulty in the long run. Life is inherently moral, and we all think constantly in moral terms.

Something as simple as driving illustrates this point. If someone cuts us off in traffic, passes us on the wrong side, or speeds past us, we might get angry. Behind that anger lies a moral judgment. We don't think that what the other driver has done is simply not to our liking. We don't merely prefer that he not drive recklessly. We think he has committed an act that is morally wrong. We think he "should not" drive that way.

That "should not" is important. It indicates our inward awareness of a moral standard that we believe should be met no matter how difficult it may be to do so. This inward sense of right and wrong is sometimes called "the moral law." Examining the implications of the moral law and how we know it extends far beyond the scope of this book. The salient point here is that life is inescapably moral, even in mundane circumstances, and that we know this intuitively.

Most of us, however, do not have a conscious mental framework for dealing with the moral complexities of life. Instead, we rely on our guts. We feel that something is right or wrong in our bodies and can't articulate why, beyond pointing to these simple impulses. For this reason, taking some time to reflect on the moral dimension of life is critical if we want to develop into people who have more to say than just that something feels wrong.

The consequences of this unreflective approach are everywhere. Acting on or forming firm opinions based on nothing more than moral prejudice destroys relationships at both the personal and political levels. Rushing to judgment without a developed system by which to form balanced and compassionate assessments erects walls that separate us from our friends, family, and acquaintances.

The political consequences of unreflective moral outrage are painfully evident in the public square. People polarized into opposing camps shriek at one another hysterically rather than seeking the kind of understanding that would allow a multi-faceted analysis of the other side's claims.

On the personal level, we are normally more vocal about those times when others have wronged us than about those times when we have wronged others. We desire justice from them, but not for them. We insist on our total innocence and their total corruption. Our impulse to defend ourselves from even the gentlest and most obviously correct moral criticism shuts down the conversation and sharing that is the lifeblood of real relationships.

Escaping this situation requires serious consideration of moral realities, of the failings of others and of ourselves. We must step back and think through the urge toward moral judgment to see if there isn't a way to refine these impulses into a more sophisticated and compassionate system.

A Quick Sketch of Ethical Approaches

Fortunately, much of this work has already been done for us. Because humans have always wrestled with moral issues, people have been thinking about these matters for a long time. This thinking has tended, in the West, to fall into three broad categories: one seeks to determine our moral duties; one judges moral actions based on their consequences; the last takes an entirely different approach and roots the solution to ethical problems in the habits of the good person.

The first of these traditions is technically referred to as deontology. It gets its name from the Greek word "deon" meaning duty. Deontological perspectives tend also to be absolutist, holding that one must do one's duty regardless of the consequences for oneself or others. Deontologists aim to find a moral principle which can guide right action in every conceivable circumstance and render a sense of moral certainty in the face of messy situations.

Many deontological approaches exist. Perhaps the most common argues that right and wrong are determined by God's commands and prohibitions. According to this view, we have a duty to do those things God has commanded and not to do what He has prohibited. God, from this perspective, is the only authority with a legitimate right to dictate the difference between right and wrong and to demand that we should obey.

Deontological views are not, however, solely for the religious. Immanuel Kant sought to create a deontological system that rooted the call of duty not in religion, but in human reason and experience. From Kant's point of view, moral principles or imperatives could be arrived at through the use of human intellectual powers. The most important of these was his "Categorical Imperative" which, in a rough paraphrase, argues that we ought not to act in ways we can't simultaneously want everyone else to act.

The primary alternative to deontological systems are consequentialist ones. While these approaches vary, their common thread is the claim that the rightness or wrongness of an action can be determined by whether or not it produces beneficial results.

Probably the most well-known of these systems is Utilitarianism. Developed in the 18th and 19th centuries by Jeremy Bentham and later by John Stuart Mill, this philosophy holds that actions must be judged according to the principle of utility, or how useful an action is for producing happiness. Over the years, philosophers working in this stream of thought have nuanced these claims, but this idea remains its base.

Most approaches to ethics in the history of Western philosophy, with a few notable exceptions, can be classified under one of these approaches. Rare is the system that is neither deontological nor consequentialist.

It is to one of these rare exceptions we now turn. This approach, originating in ancient Greece, emphasizes not so much the question of whether individual actions are right or wrong, but the question, "What is a good person?" This small shift of emphasis makes a big difference. Rather than a search for a knowable, universally applicable moral principle or set of moral rules, focusing on personal virtue launches us into a process of trial and error, learning and habituation. Because this approach spotlights the connection between the inner characteristics of the actor and the moral status of the action, we might say that virtue ethics is more psychological than the other approaches.

Rooted in the thinking of Aristotle, virtue theory stresses the need for moral education, for the cultivation of certain habits of heart and mind. The goal of this practice is a state Aristotle called "Eudaimonia," a word often translated as "happiness." Happiness here, though, is no mere fleeting mental condition, but an ongoing state of flourishing in which a person's capacities for reason and enjoyment are fulfilled.

The promise of this fulfillment relates to the practice of individual virtue through the assumption that reality has an inherent moral structure. Behind the call to pursue certain character traits lies the notion that by pursuing these traits, a human being puts himself in line with the underlying moral skeleton of human relationships. So, a person we call "fair" is so because "fairness" is a real thing that the virtuous person exemplifies in his actions. The character of the virtuous person, in this view, is a reflection, on a small scale, of that larger set of moral realities I called "the moral law." The moral order is a round hole, and it is through the practice of virtue we take our square selves, round off the edges, and fit ourselves for the invisible order that governs human realities.

Virtue, as conceived by Aristotle, was the mean between extremes[1]. He thought virtuous action consisted of the ability to choose actions that fell in the middle of a spectrum. One famous example of this is bravery. Bravery, Aristotle thought, was the mean between the extremes of foolhardiness, a habit of proceeding without taking stock of risks, and cowardice, a habit of fleeing all danger.

However, in the centuries since Aristotle, "virtue" has come to have a more colloquial, less technical meaning. When we use the word, we don't necessarily mean "the mean between extremes." Instead, in modern usage, when we say virtue, we mean something like "a good trait to have" or a trait that indicates an overall good character." In this book, I will use "virtue" in this modern, casual way rather than in the strict Aristotelian sense.

---

1. Aristotle, *Nichomachean Ethics*, 31.

Common Good

The Ethics of Everyday Life

All this philosophy can seem like abstract and rarefied stuff. It's not. Rather, the matters touched on here have much to do with the patterns of our everyday living. Whether we take a strictly deontological or consequentialist approach to determining right from wrong, or whether we look at things from a virtue ethics perspective makes a difference. We cannot simply avoid employing one of these approaches. Daily life demands constant moral decision making, and that demands we have an approach for making such decisions.

This becomes clear upon a moment's reflection. Daily life is hard. Our difficulties form the context of and the impetus for our moral decision-making. Our interactions with friends, spouses, children, work associates, and strangers constantly require assessing right and wrong. Our choices in these relationships both reveal and form who we are. It is in the crucible of our daily moral challenges that our character is formed.

Take a common example. Most parents who have been home from work all day with their children have found it a mixed blessing. Imagine this situation. After several hours of listening to her children play loudly, argue with one another, and whine because there is nothing good to eat in the house, our hypothetical mother may begin to find herself on edge. Tensions, often indiscernible to children, who tend to be oblivious about such things, grow. Feelings reach a boiling point when a child needs to be told for the thousandth time to pick up her coat off the living room floor and return it to the place where it hangs.

What a parent does in this situation will depend on his conception of moral reality. A strict deontologist might mentally scan the list of divine commands and prohibitions looking for guidance on how to best interact with his children. A consequentialist will think through what action would make life better for everyone. A virtue ethicist will ask what a virtuous parent should do in this situation.

The parent who holds to a virtue ethics paradigm will not merely think about consequences or duties, though both of these may play a part in choosing his response. He will also think about the moral education his child is receiving. He will be concerned with her practical habits in the areas of obedience to legitimate authority, care for property, and orderliness of life. His response to his child will be more than punishment for having contravened her duty nor will he attempt to merely create a bad consequence for the child. A virtue-oriented parent sees these moments as part of a child's ongoing moral education, the process that builds the soul.

This example illustrates two important strengths about the virtue ethics approach and why such an approach serves as the basis for this book. Virtue ethics, because it stresses the overall moral development of the individual, encompasses concerns about both duties and consequences. The virtuous person is one who possesses the wisdom necessary to weigh these factors and to determine how to pursue one's duties even when unpleasant consequences are likely to follow. Rather than making either duty or consequence the final criteria for moral decision-making, virtue ethics acknowledges the importance of both and offers us an image of the person who balances them well.

Our story of the flustered parent is just one example of the myriad moral complexities we face in daily life. Again and again we find ourselves looking for the right response to situations that arise. For most of us, this search is unconscious. Making this search conscious is important because, as virtue theory insists, our moral behavior is largely a matter of habit. We cannot possibly engage in deep reflection on each moral situation we face daily. Instead, we cultivate a series of habits to see us through. These habits eventually form the core of our self. Over the long run, the habits we develop determine the quality of our relationships and of our self-understanding—yet another reason why these matters matter. To allow this process to remain wholly unconscious is to surrender our freedom to choose the quality of our character and relationships. Far from being an abstract academic exercise reserved for intellectuals, moral reflection is a practical means for determining the trajectory of our lives.

The second reason this book takes a virtue-oriented approach is because, as has been said, virtue ethics stresses moral education. Inherent in an ethical system that emphasizes moral education is the promise that it is never too late. At any point, an individual can begin to pursue virtue. Through a combination of intellectual reflection and embodied practice, any person can move from being less virtuous to more virtuous.

We can also teach others to be virtuous. Sometimes, as with our children, this teaching can be explicit and may involve measures of discipline and even punishment. More often, we teach others to be virtuous through our example. Through our own pursuit of virtue, we breathe life into others' desires to do the same. For this reason, virtue is most effectively pursued in community. When virtuous people seek to become more virtuous in one another's company, they can create an upward spiral of moral learning.

About This Book

Since ongoing moral education is a central value in a virtue ethics paradigm, it's no surprise that such a paradigm would give rise to this book. One method of moral education is to reflect on various vices and virtues. With the goal of translating insight into daily practice.

This book aims to help. Rather than seeking to be another academic text on ethics, this book aims to offer reflections on common vices and virtues and the many ways those character traits play out in our daily lives. In addition to this, you'll find short reflections on the nature of vice and virtue themselves. The particular character traits mentioned in this volume were chosen for various reasons. Some, like discipline, sloth and love, were chosen because they are fundamental to many other vices and virtues. Others were chosen because while they are important, they are much more rarely remarked on. When, for example, did you last hear a thorough discussion of gossip or of domestic virtue?

This book is, by no means, an exhaustive examination of every possible character trait. There is more to say on these topics than could ever fit into a single volume. When you close the back cover of this book, you may not have a complete understanding of your own moral system or a comprehensive ethical philosophy. There are many resources that can help you with that, if that is what you seek.

Rather, the purpose of these essays is to open space in the reader's mind and heart. For some, these essays may constitute an initial attempt to think seriously about the content examined here. For others, I hope to cast new light on these central and ancient concepts. Failing that, perhaps I can present well-known truths in a way that connects with a new and often bereft generation.

These essays seek to address the mind, of course, but to penetrate more deeply than any merely mental exercise. They aim to inform in the deepest sense, to shape the inner and, ultimately, the outer lives of their readers. They aim to penetrate to the moral center of the individual and to make such an impression there that, even once their words are forgotten, their outline will remain.

To aim at this place and for these reasons is not the job of philosophy alone, but of wisdom, and that is what this volume seeks to impart. Wisdom, in all her forms, is apprehended not by mind nor by heart alone but by the soul. And it is the health of the soul, of course, that is ultimately at stake in our daily navigation between vice and virtue.

2

Understanding Vice

A Shortage of Categories

MOST OF US, IF we think about it at all, think of evil as acts that are especially heinous. We use the word for actions like those in the September 11, 2001, attacks which took the lives of more than 3,000 and caused incalculable suffering. Sometimes we hear about a particularly violent crime, perhaps a crime against a child, and we don't hesitate to call it evil.

We are right to do so. Those acts are evil, and it is good for us to call them so. Our recognition of the evil in these instances is evidence of our inner awareness of the moral law. If we had no inner sense that human beings should not behave in these ways, we would have no motivation for condemning them.

But, we do have this inner sense. If we are sensitive to it, we will see that it is always active, forever signaling us about the moral quality of our experience. Our inner moral sense doesn't flare up just in those situations where something egregious is going on.

Few of us have a difficult time seeing how extremely damaging behaviors fall short of our inward ideal. But we have a harder time acknowledging and articulating a moral diagnosis of more pedestrian failings. We know that not every failure to live up to the inner sense of what we should be is evil. Though we often lack the categories necessary to describe these intuitions, we feel an undeniable sense of discomfort when we fail to meet these ideals.

To talk intelligibly or helpfully about these more routine failures requires more categories than simply good and evil. We cannot sort every human action easily into these binary categories. We need more baskets into which to toss the wide variety of attitudes, beliefs, behaviors and choices we encounter.

The Need for Vice as a Moral Category

This is why a discussion of vice matters. Vice does not mean evil. Vice is a category for talking about these everyday failures that while unproductive and perhaps hurtful do not rise to the level of moral destructiveness implied the word "evil." Understanding that our behavior and choices can be afflicted by vice allows us to be more compassionate with ourselves and others. When we understand vice, we can own our negative behaviors without having to assume for ourselves the moniker of "evil."

When we grasp the category of "vice," we can accept imperfection more graciously when we encounter it in ourselves and others. Seeing that being human means consistent failure to realize our moral potential, consistent failure to be as good as we could possibly be, we can release ourselves and others from the burden of expecting us all to do otherwise. A good understanding of vice puts these daily failures into proper perspective.

Vice and Human Potential

This does not mean vice is trivial or does not merit taking seriously. Since the fulfillment of the human being is intimately tied to moral ideals, any instance of moral failure, however slight, is an indication that we have not attained the full measure of our identity. We must take vice seriously because it represents a trap, a trap into which, if we fall, we will languish, never becoming that which we long to become. Vice, in this way, is the enemy of human happiness. And that alone is reason to take it seriously.

Too few of us do. Most of us, most of the time, pour enormous energy into not looking at our vices. We distract ourselves. We deny reality. We blame others and justify our shortcomings based upon our circumstances. Ceasing to do these things is the first step toward weeding vice out of our hearts and moving toward virtue.

Unfortunately, this process is not easy, and our culture doesn't help. Our cultural practices now seem geared toward taking this process of self-avoidance and ramping it up to the highest possible degree.

Understanding Vice

In modern American society almost everyone takes an overpowering addiction to constant, intense stimulation as normal. We assume that life devoid of a single moment of silence is what we were intended for. Our distraction is constant. Most of us carry in our pockets a machine designed specifically to distract us from those moments of loneliness, of discomfort or just dullness that surface many times each day.

All this distraction prevents serious reflection on our character, on the vices to which we easily succumb and the virtues toward which we ought to be striving. To know our moral character and to face our faults requires sustained thought and awareness, and the pre-condition for both of those is silence.

How We Avoid Facing Our Vices

And silence, because of its potential for leading us into confrontation with our shortcomings, is what we avoid. Certainly, our distractions offer us positive, if temporary, rewards, but we are drawn to them as much by what they allow us to avoid as by the rewards they offer. We do not want to face ourselves, and our entire society now conspires to help us do so.

But distraction is far from the only means by which we avoid looking at ourselves. We find other ways. For example, we also often simply deny reality. Human beings always have, and a penchant for denial is built into our nature. Our tendency to refuse to acknowledge what is right in front of us is among the most devastating forms of self-avoidance. When we cannot acknowledge our vices, their power grows, and as their power grows, so does the damage they inflict.

Denial, a defense mechanism in which we refuse to acknowledge realities for which there is good evidence, is a particularly powerful means for disavowing our shortcomings because it allows us to live an imaginary life, to live as if choices do not have consequences. This is most obvious perhaps with vices of self-indulgence and excess. The story of the alcoholic whose professional life and relationships are being ruined by his drinking, but who nevertheless blames everyone and everything but his choice to drink for this series of catastrophes, is a well-known example of denial.

Others examples are more subtle. We can deny that our overeating is causing our health problems. We can deny that our rage is causing people to distance themselves from us. We can pretend our refusal to get adequate sleep isn't making us irritable and sluggish at work. We can tell ourselves over and over again that we'd be so much happier if only the children would behave and let us get on with the really important stuff of life. In all these situations, we deny core truths about our moral state.

Every instance of denial has a common root. That root is the inner fear of seeing ourselves as we are. We much prefer to see ourselves as we imagine we are. When others refuse to play along with our imaginary world, our fear can easily become anger at them for exposing the game we are playing. If possible, many of us would play this denial game until the day we die. Yet, the quest to become fulfilled and peaceful demands that we do the opposite, that we face our shortcomings squarely even if that means enduring some temporary discomfort.

Those who aren't in denial may just resort to being defensive. Many of us remain stuck in the grip of our vices simply because we have developed the reflexive and automatic habit of defending them. We act as though we have an absolute right to them and that others' complaints about them are, in some way, a grievous violation of our freedom.

We do not see that blaming others for our shortcomings, rather than being a means to freedom, is a major factor in our continued bondage. When we blame others for our vices and failures, we perpetuate the habits of mind and heart that keep us stuck. We cannot move forward because we have convinced ourselves that others are to blame for our failures and that in order for us to do better, others must change.

The problem lies not in acknowledging that others have failed us. The problem lies in clinging with all our power to the idea that others' failures somehow justify our own. Too often, we hold others to an absolute moral scale while grading ourselves on the curve. We make allowances for our own imperfections that we do not extend to others.

If we allow ourselves to judge our own actions in light of the poor actions of others, we can always make ourselves out to be a victim. And, we believe, no one has the right to tell a victim that he needs to change. Too often, we demand justice from others as the precondition for our own decision to act more justly. The end result is neither justice nor change, but continued frustration of our impulse toward growth.

Taking Responsibility for Our Character is the Key To Growth

No amount of demanding others change actually produces change in others. If we wait until they are perfect to begin a quest to be free of our vices, we will never begin. Instead, we take responsibility for our character regardless of whether others are willing to take responsibility for theirs. This step alone produces great inner freedom. As soon as we cease seeing ourselves as leaves blown about by the winds of others' choices and instead assume the responsibility inherent in being an active, choice-making being, we feel a greater sense of both stability and possibility.

Assuming responsibility for one's choices regardless of others' behavior is frightening. We are afraid that doing so will open the door for others to harm us, to remind us of our failures mercilessly. We fear that if we own, rather than deny, our flaws, we will be opening ourselves up to unnecessary pain.

In truth, owning our flaws weakens others' power over us and allows us to develop greater awareness and compassion. Ceasing to reflexively deny our failings is like lifting weights. It makes us stronger. As a result, we grow strong enough to make choices that benefit us including the choice to disengage from people who, because they will not own their flaws, cannot create fruitful relationships.

Overcoming Vice Is the Path to Growth

Whether we avoid taking responsibility for our vices through distraction, denial or defensiveness, we will never begin the journey to rid ourselves of them until we can admit that our vices are real, and that they hold us back from being something nearer that ideal version of ourselves that haunts our minds.

But admitting our vices alone does not free us from them. We must also be able to name and to relinquish them. In other words, if we desire to be free of a vice, we must first know what a vice is.

Many people think of vices as surface level behaviors, things like smoking, eating or drinking too much, gossip, overspending and so on. Those people are certainly right. Vices do have external, behavioral components we can see and touch. Overcoming our vices necessarily implies a change in behavior.

But there is more. The undue focus on the external has contributed to the popular notion that the word vice means something naughty but not very serious. When we hear vice discussed in popular culture, the word is used to denote some behavior that is pleasurable but which has almost no actual harmful consequences. A housewife in a television show might, for example, refer to her habit of eating a chocolate every afternoon as "her little vice."

But vice is serious. Vice infects more than just our behavior. Vice also shapes our character. There are a whole list of vices of the heart and mind that are rarely mentioned in contemporary culture. When was the last time you heard a serious discussion of frivolousness or of sloth?

Vice is the habit of choosing attitudes and behaviors that inhibit our growth or that contradict our inner sense of moral reality. We can have behavioral habits, certainly, but we also have habits of heart and mind that determine those patterns.

Addressing our behavioral vices has some value. Of course, we will be healthier if we stop smoking. We will likely be happier if we adopt an exercise routine. But focusing exclusively on behavior misses the deeper point. That is why this is not a book about how to quit smoking, how to eat less, or how to be less angry while driving, but rather an attempt to offer some helpful reflections on the attitudes that underly these behaviors.

If we are not merely to be free of negative and costly behaviors, but really to be a version of ourselves more in line with our ideal, we must work below the surface. We must seek to cultivate habits of thinking and feeling that are appropriate to that better version of ourselves. Attempting to change our behavior only without changing the underlying attitudes is one reason people so often fail in their attempts at bettering themselves.

At its worst, this approach leads people into a kind of anxious behavior monitoring where the goal is not really to be better versions of themselves, but only to seem so to others. Eventually, the mask grows too heavy and, sooner or later, slips, revealing to both others and to ourselves that the most crucial work remains undone.

Dealing with Guilt and Shame

The topics of guilt and shame necessarily accompany any discussion of personal vice, and demand to be addressed here. Handling our feelings about confronting our vices can be unpleasant. It helps if we separate guilt and shame.

Understanding Vice

Guilt is the objective condition of having fallen short of the standard, of not having been the person we know we are obligated to be. Shame, on the other hand, is the notion that guilt somehow disqualifies us from receiving respect from others and from ourselves, that our guilt has made us unacceptable, or that others have a right to punish us for our failures.

Because everyone fails to live out his moral duties, everyone is guilty. Because everyone fails to live out his duties in multiple ways daily, everyone is equally guilty. Guilt is inescapable. Shame is not. Everyone is guilty, but not everyone is ashamed.

Those who struggle with shame when it comes to looking at their vices should take solace in the idea of universal human guilt. Because everyone fails morally, there is very little point in trying to create a moral hierarchy. The questions of whether one person is morally better than another is ultimately pointless. The point is not to cower in shame in front of those we might consider our moral betters, but to begin wherever we are to reckon with the vices ingrained in us.

As we do so, our sense of shame will begin to dissipate. Self-contempt will be replaced by self-respect. The power of previous misdeeds will fade as new, better habits take root. As we begin to see the deeper changes we've been cultivating begin coming to fruition, our hearts will lighten. Those corners once haunted by shame will be swept clean and finally be occupied, rather than by shame and self-loathing, by a greater capacity for compassion and forgiveness. This freedom and light however, are a reward reserved only for those brave enough to look their vices right in their dark and ugly faces. Now is the time.

3

Self-Indulgence

Desire and the Human Situation

To be human is to want. Desire is our constant companion. We are born wanting food and warmth and comfort. As we grow, our desires change but never leave us. Sometimes, we are conscious of very acute desires, perhaps for money or for fame or for sex. Other times, we suffer a chronic low-grade wanting. We fill the moments of our lives imagining how wonderful life would be if we got whatever we think we want, or scheming ways to lay our hands on it.

The result is an increase in misery. Desire, whether its objects are distinct or only vaguely considered, tends to focus us on what we don't have. In the grip of strong desire, we blind ourselves to the riches of the present moment, dismissing it as inferior to a moment in which our desire might finally be satisfied. This mindset leads us to see the present moment as a mere stepping stone to some other moment in which our desires will be finally gratified.

Our desiring nature leads us to all manner of unpleasant inner experiences: jealousy, anger, anxiety, a general sense of disquiet and meaninglessness. Most never notice this. Desiring is so much in our nature and so encouraged by contemporary consumer culture that we take it as the normal course of things. To ask whether our basic experience of desire might somehow be harming us or leaving us unfulfilled seems a shocking breach of consumerist orthodoxy.

Self-Indulgence

Nevertheless the shocking truth is that our ceaseless wanting leaves us empty. Nothing seems to be enough. No sooner do we acquire one object for which we have longed than does our desire turn to the next. This tendency is so powerful, we can easily remain in the grip of the "just-one-more-thing" delusion all our lives.

To desire in itself is not bad, but our untutored nature is a riot of longing that, unless properly brought to heel, ensures our pain. Turning our desiring nature to a good and fruitful end requires escaping the "just-one-more-thing" delusion. The first step toward freedom is accepting that few things truly satisfy, and then focusing on acquiring those things and allowing ourselves to be satisfied.

The alternative, and the strategy most people opt for, is a life of self-indulgence. The end result of this choice is that our world shrinks, our relationships wither, opportunities pass us by. As each of these things happen, our connection to what makes life meaningful becomes more tenuous until we find ourselves full of every pleasure but the pleasure of knowing what pleasures mean. We end up slaves to our internal impulses with no ability to connect to anything that orders and lends meaning to our behavior.

The Characteristics of Self-Indulgence

Understanding why we do this is tricky. First, we must understand that merely possessing a desiring nature does not constitute self-indulgence. Our desiring nature is universal, and yet self-indulgence is not. If having a desiring nature automatically entailed self-indulgence, there would be no such thing as a person who was not self-indulgent. Clearly, a desiring nature and being self-indulgent are not identical.

To get a better grasp on what self-indulgence is, it's helpful to describe some its characteristics. Three essential traits define self-indulgence. First, self-indulgence requires ease. The self-indulgent look for the path of least resistance. They seek no long-term goal, not even the amassing of a fortune, that would require them to overcome any real obstacles. In this way, self-indulgence is a close cousin to sloth.

Second, self-indulgence is characterized by excess, especially excess engagement with a pleasure that is easily obtained. The self-indulgent are not people who enjoy pleasures only obtained through serious work. One of the most pernicious aspects of self-indulgence is that it limits the scope of the pleasures one can enjoy. A life of self-indulgence pushes pleasures like a feeling of accomplishment and the increasing self-respect that comes from achieving a goal, outside the realm of possibility.

Third, self-indulgence is characterized by immediacy. The self-indulgent are looking for pleasure now. Self-indulgent people do not have a plan. They are experts at surrendering long-term gain for short-term fun. One more drink, they think, won't cost them much tomorrow. Because the true costs of eating a bag of cheeseburgers won't come for years, they reason, it's fine to consume them now. "A bill that will come due in the future need never be paid" is their motto.

It's easy to take a simplistic and judgmental approach toward self-indulgence, but that will not do. Too often, we imagine that the real problem here is merely one of will. If the person trapped in patterns of self-indulgence would only try harder, she could put these patterns away and move on to a more productive and meaningful life. When this doesn't happen, the tendency is to respond with either criticism or abandonment. Many of us seem to imagine that the way to help another get free of self-indulgent behavior is to criticize or nag. We may be tempted to step in and serve as her conscience, constantly reminding her of her shortcomings and telling her how she could do better.

This accomplishes nothing. In fact, this approach often pushes people more deeply into their bad habits, resulting in the opposite of what the critic originally hoped for. Many people who struggle with self-indulgence do so as a means of escaping criticism and social pressure. Adding our judgements to the negative stimuli they are seeking to avoid only drives them deeper into their preferred coping mechanisms.

When criticism and nagging don't work, walking away from the relationship may seem the next option. This is not always unreasonable. Self-indulgent habits do take a toll on relationships. Consistent self-indulgence erects barriers between people and drives others away. In fact, keeping others at a distance is often one of the benefits self-indulgent people accrue from their behavior.

When possible though, it's often better to remain in relationships with the self-indulgent. Like everyone else, self-indulgent people need the security of long-term relationships in which to process through the underlying hurts and false beliefs that led to their self-indulgent patterns in the first place. In cases where a relationship with a person stuck in self-indulgent patterns is not abusive or otherwise detrimental, continuing to relate to that person with patience and love can go a long way toward helping him change. Besides, everyone needs a good example.

The Inner Dynamics of Self-Indulgence

Criticism and abandonment in the lives of the self-indulgent don't always come from others. Often, self-indulgent people are quite critical and abandoning of themselves. Most people with self-indulgent habits are aware enough to know their behavior is a problem, but perhaps not aware enough to know how to change. They too sometimes buy into the "if you try harder you'll succeed" mentality. So, for self-indulgent people, life becomes a seesaw of indulgence and self-criticism, a relentless and unproductive back and forth of indulging the self, criticizing the self, and then trying to abandon the self through greater indulgence. Better than either criticism or abandonment is to understand the inner dynamics of self-indulgent behavior and more sustainable approaches to change.

On one level, it's not hard to understand the appeal of life in pursuit of ease. We all want things to be easy. In fact, we long for ease so much that when it's denied us, we can become bitter.

In spite of how much we long for things to be easy, things are usually difficult. Again and again, we all confront daily, in ways large and small, the fundamental brokenness of the world. Chaos and entropy must constantly be held at bay. In spite of our best efforts, they seep through. The car breaks down. The hotel lost our reservation. We get sick at the worst possible time.

If we have the right kind of inner resources, if we have goals that motivate us and we have a sense that the fight is worth it, that rewards are regular and sufficient we keep going. Under those conditions, we find we can press on in the face of the continuous pressures and challenges of life.

But such conditions are not present for everyone. Sometimes, self-indulgent behavior is an attempt to compensate for the lack of the factors that allow us to press on in the face of resistance. Self-indulgent people, in their hunger for those things that make life bearable, seek short cuts. While everyone needs a break, a vacation, some down time, people who struggle with self-indulgence seek to make vacation the majority of life, and in so doing neglect the work necessary for both personal fulfillment and making valuable contributions to others.

For these people, something has gone wrong, and the the problems may be located in multiple areas. People who have an inordinate longing for ease lack the inner resources necessary to deal successfully with the uneasy world. I hear often from people online who struggle with intense anxiety, sometimes in social situations, sometimes at work. They lack the inner confidence necessary to set boundaries for themselves and to engage with others in ways that allow them to feel safe and valued.

In light of the demands of living, some people attempt to withdraw into a life devoted to creating as much ease as possible. This means avoiding situations where much will be demanded of them. Undertaking a challenging career or even getting serious training is too much for them. They simply cannot cope with the feeling that others are depending on them or that their work matters. They may fear disappointing others or suffering consequences should they perform poorly.

Building relationships is also difficult for such people. We all have expectations of those we are close to. We all have needs we want others to meet. For self-indulgent people addicted to ease, the expectations of others can be either suffocating or terrifying. They may worry about losing a relationship if they fail to meet the other person's standards. They may feel the other person is treating them unfairly by having any expectations at all.

The result of all this is that such people avoid meaningful work and meaningful relationships and thus the possibility of a meaningful life. They avoid fulfilling their professional and creative potential by choosing the path of least resistance, perhaps taking positions whose work is far below what they are capable of. They often lead lives of loneliness because they avoid getting close to others.

The antidote to their situation is not merely to try harder not to be lazy, but to cultivate awareness of their inner strength. Starting small can help too. Facing small challenges is the path to uncovering one's inner strength. Like a weightlifter who gradually increases the number of pounds on his barbell, tackling small problems makes stronger people whose inner muscles are weak.

People who struggle with a self-indulgent lifestyle might also have trouble connecting to goals. Perhaps their hearts have been so seared by disappointment that conjuring a goal is beyond them. Experience has worn them down so much that even summoning the strength to imagine a meaningful goal seems beyond their ability.

Self-indulgent people may have learned that life does not return rewards commensurate with the amount of struggle achieving a goal requires.

Self-Indulgence

They may feel cheated. Why struggle when struggle returns too little, and it's so easy to sit on the couch inhaling fast food and binge-watching Netflix?

Believing this is partially warranted. The truth is that rewards are not equally distributed in the world. Many people work tirelessly for very little and others seem to prosper almost in spite of their efforts. Not much living is required to see that hard work and diligence alone do not always produce bounty.

Eventually the disappointment this reality breeds paired with the instant gratification easy pleasures offer can dampen a person's ability to connect to any goals. The less we do, the less that seems worth doing until we arrive at the point where achieving any goal seems impossible.

Changing Self-Indulgent Patterns

Overcoming self-indulgence then, requires both a mental reset and a change in behavioral patterns. The assumption that because rewards are unevenly distributed in the world achieving personal goals is not worth the effort simply doesn't stand up to scrutiny. Freeing oneself from the grip of this belief will require a conscious effort to identify where it shows up in our thinking. When it pops up, we must replace it with a different, better thought, one that justifies the effort we are making.

But even more important than changing our thinking is simply deciding to act as if our goals are worth the efforts they demand. If we set very small goals that require only a bit more effort than we might normally exert, the momentum we create in accomplishing them can carries us a long way toward releasing our self-indulgent patterns.

It is not mere momentum nor will that allows us to transcend our self-indulgent patterns though. One reason many people remain in the grip of self-indulgent habits is simply that they rely on will power as the first and last resource for change. Will power will always give out when your will is weak. In truth, a weak will does not lead to self-indulgence; self-indulgence leads to a weak will. As we seek to make changes, we notice our will to uphold them strengthens. Eventually, a new, less indulgent lifestyle emerges without strain on our part.

What the self-indulgent miss is that ease, excess and immediacy ultimately do not satisfy. Our missed opportunities haunt us. Our withered potential aches but does not die. Try as we might we cannot ignore the pain of progress denied. Rather, it is the sense of moving toward our ideal

Common Good

self which comforts us in the difficulties we must voluntarily undertake to reach our goals. Meaning and lasting satisfaction are possible, but the hard part of the journey toward them always comes first. Denying this truth is part of the prison we build for ourselves, and only to the degree that we accept it will we finally be free.

4

Frivolousness

A Picture of the Frivolous

A FEW YEARS AGO, I attended a meeting of a local homeschool group. As the men leading it assembled on stage, each of them wore some sort of ridiculous hat. Don't imagine something as tasteful as a baseball cap with moose ears. No, think Dr. Seuss instead. These men, the leaders of a group devoted to helping parents usher their children to maturity, deemed it appropriate to open the school year by each trotting out something that would have been more fitting on the head of the Cat in the Hat.

What inspired this choice of haberdashery I don't know, but I do know that it was part of an overall ethos in our culture that is suspicious of seriousness, of gravity, and of maturity. The spirit of our age eschews these things in an attempt to make all things fun, or rather, to make all things funny. Perhaps these men were afraid to stand in front of the group and present themselves to us as leaders who took the purpose of the group with utmost seriousness and who, in return, expected to be taken seriously.

There is, after all, a strain of thought in our culture that sees all seriousness as pretension, all expectation that people will take one another seriously as an oppressive rigidity which confines the vivacious spirit of relationships within burdensome formality.

This trend makes frivolousness the default mode of being in our culture. Our relationships as well as our thinking tend to be marked by triviality, an orientation toward pleasure above all else, and lack of purpose. Together, these amount to frivolousness.

Understanding Frivolousness and Maturity

It's important to begin with an understanding that leaving behind frivolousness does not mean leaving behind joy, humor, or even necessarily jokes, pranks or clever stunts. The opposite of frivolousness is not dourness, but maturity. Ceasing to be frivolous means leaving behind a mode of being in which life itself is seen as a joke whose peak is a few moments of ironic humor.

Consider what maturity is. Human beings, just like plants, are beings that must grow from their nascent into their mature forms. Each year, in our garden, our family plants seeds we know will, under the right circumstances, become mature plants yielding fruit.

Human beings are subject to a similar process. Our ultimate potential lies dormant in each of us. As we mature, just as a plant grows from a seedling to adult plant, we move from a cute bundle of potential toward the realization of the fullness of all our gifts.

By moving through the maturation process, we become more of what we are meant to be. But unlike a plant, our potential can only ever be approached, never fully realized. Human beings, because we are infinitely more complex than plants, can never exhaust our potential no matter how much we may have matured.

Still, this maturation process demands that we become serious. As children, we have a hard time estimating what's at stake in our decision making. If we are fortunate children, we are led toward higher states of thinking, feeling and behaving. In a nurturing situation for a child, life is dominated by play, and a sense of carefree rest in his parents' love and provision.

In this situation, we can afford to make mistakes. Risk is limited and losses we incur are often mitigated by our parents. If, in playing too roughly with a favorite toy, we break it, kind parents might replace it or teach us how to earn another one. Our losses are rarely permanent in these early days.

As we grow however, our decisions involve more risk. As teenagers, we might, for example, learn to drive a car, a privilege that moves us into a new arena of responsibility. We have gone from the protected world of childhood where our decisions rarely involved the possibility of serious outcomes to a world where our actions behind the wheel can mean life or death.

The increased possibility of very serious outcomes from our decisions should mark a corresponding move toward serious thinking and behavior. Increased risk of negative outcomes should mean increased capacity to avoid choices likely to bring them about.

Frivolousness

Just as we ought to move toward a more serious and responsible attitude as we mature, we ought also to move toward an increased seriousness of purpose. As children, our consciousnesses are often consumed by the immediate. We become absorbed in the moment. When we want something, we want it now! As we age, we acquire a greater ability to look into the future and see how our immediate choices may have long-term effects. At the same time, our power to create serious consequences for good or for ill increases.

Along with this greater ability to shape reality should come a greater determination to direct our newly discovered power to certain ends. We eventually realize that if we consistently exercise our power in certain ways, outcomes become more predictable. We figure out that if we get up and go for a run every day, our aerobic capacity will increase. We begin to grasp that if we work dutifully and consistently on drawing exercises, we will eventually produce works of art which make our skill evident.

As we become more confident in our ability to make things happen, we begin to plan the conditions we hope to bring into reality over the long haul. If all goes well, these insights bring about an increased seriousness of purpose. We ought to grow more serious about the goals and plans we are working toward, consistently turning positive ideas into valuable reality.

Doing this is not easy. As we seek to accomplish our purposes, we will face many forms of difficulty: the limits of our physical bodies, the complexities of navigating organizations, the wills of uncooperative people. All these can stand in our way.

Regardless of the form in which challenges to our plans make themselves felt, they are problems for us. So, along with a growing seriousness of purpose should come a growing seriousness about persevering in the face of problems. Without this kind of seriousness, our energy gets dissipated and our purposes thwarted.

And so, we can say the types of seriousness we acquire as we grow: seriousness about avoiding negative outcomes, seriousness about creating positive outcomes, and seriousness about persevering in the face of problems are hallmarks of the maturity. When we meet people who embody these, we sense that we are in the presence of a mature person.

Understanding The Unserious

These seriousnesses, however, are not present in everyone. It's always been that way. Individuals who lack seriousness of purpose or who cannot grasp the seriousness of the consequences of their behavior have always been part of our world.

This situation now has reached epidemic proportions. Everywhere we see the rejection of the kind of seriousness that has previously characterized mature adults. We see this in the behavior and attitudes of adults who spend all day playing video games and in the spectacle of the homeschool group meeting I described. The real problem with this behavior is not that it is weird or irreverent, but that is a frustration of the normal pattern of human maturation. To escape this cultural pattern we must know what constitutes frivolousness and learn to avoid it.

It's easy to get confused about frivolousness. Many other character qualities bear a surface similarity to it. Humorousness, gaiety, and simple gregariousness all can look like frivolousness to those unaccustomed to distinguishing between them. Before we look at the inner dynamics of frivolousness, let's establish what frivolousness is not.

Frivolousness is not humorousness. Humorousness, the ability to greet the difficulties of life with an attitude that lightens and palliates them, is the province of the mature adult. The absence of humor is a sign of the inward-looking self-regard that characterizes the adolescent. Facing the inherent contradictions and ironies of human travails and articulating those in ways that lift the spirits of others is serious business. Because humor serves such a serious function, it can never be frivolous.

Celebration is also not frivolous. Celebration is a necessary part of individual and communal experience. Many occasions in life call for celebration. At such times, a refusal to celebrate would be a mark of immaturity and self-absorption. Celebrations, with their concomitant light-heartedness, mark the passing of important and serious milestones of human life, whether those are weddings, religious holidays, anniversaries or retirements. Sometimes, even deaths are marked by a kind of celebration.

Irony is also not frivolousness. Cultivating a view of life that accepts its absurdities and contradictions is simply a way of trudging through the hard parts. In fact, some develop an unusually ironic sense of humor because they take the challenges life presents so seriously. Seeing the absurdity in our situations, even those with potentially very important outcomes, can sometimes help us to press on when we feel like giving up.

Even the desire to be funny is not inherently frivolous. A desire to entertain others in social situations, when it complements a larger set of social skills, can be an important mode of service. When the desire to make others laugh grows from a desire to lighten the burdens of others, it is noble.

Frivolous people are not necessarily funny people. To be consistently funny requires practice and sensitivity to others. This desire to bring levity to others' difficult circumstances is a serious purpose. Frivolous people by definition don't have this. It is an irony of the moral world that frivolous people are often too frivolous to be funny, too unserious to offer others the blessings of good humor.

A regular practice of refreshment and entertainment is also not frivolous. We get tired. Our bodies run out of gas and must be refilled. This limits our capacity for serious work. Once we have reached these limits and must cease work, we long to engage in some form of recreation. If we do this to fortify ourselves in order to return to the pursuit of our serious purpose, then this period of refreshment, even if it is filled with light activities is part of our larger serious purpose.

We also become emotionally and spiritually tired. We long for an experience with a reality different from and better than our experience of this world. We long to put aside our burdens for a few minutes and simply enjoy a story or spectacle which requires little of us. Weary people can only receive. The disciplined use of entertainment opportunities allows us to do this.

It's not hard to see why people might confuse these things with frivolousness, but to remain in this confusion is not to look deeply enough. The central distinction here is not between people who enjoy themselves and those who don't. It is between those who enjoy themselves by engaging in humor, celebration and other light-hearted bits of life in a larger context of overall seriousness about life and those who pursue these things as means to escape the demand to mature. The key to knowing whether a person is frivolous or not lies in assessing their underlying attitudes not in merely observing their behavior.

Once we can say what it means to be frivolous, we need to be able to say what it means to be serious. Just as it might be easy to confuse frivolousness with gaiety, it is easy to confuse seriousness with dourness, or worse, anger and resentment.

The dour person, like the frivolous person, is not serious. It is entirely possible for a person to be dour, negative and grumpy because he is full of small self-centeredness and a sense of his fundamental superiority to his neighbor. The man who sits out the party when the party is serious business has no business pretending he is serious. He is instead simply withdrawn from life and therefore withdrawn from the seriousness of its purpose.

Dour people often assume their dour stance because they need to feel superior. Misjudging the celebrations or good humor of others is a convenient way to achieve this goal. By looking down on people having a good time, he can position himself, at least in his own mind, as someone above them who would never stoop so low as to have a laugh with his friends. This may chiefly be because he has no friends and no capacity for laughter, and therefore giving up such occasions amount to an easy sacrifice for him.

Just as the frivolous person does not take life seriously and thereby handicaps his ability to make a real contribution, so the dour person fails to take seriously his obligation to make a contribution to others, especially when doing so would require stepping out of his protective shell.

Where Our Frivolousness Comes From

Now that we have a grasp of what both frivolousness and seriousness are and are not, we can begin to look at where the penchant for frivolousness so dominant in our culture comes from. Let's begin with obvious examples.

The anecdote I relayed at the beginning of this chapter of men all wearing silly hats to oversee the meeting of a homeschool group was a good example. Other, less obvious, instances can be found in of a couple of our cultural stereotypes. Let's begin at the less motivated end.

The image of the young man with no prospects, no job, unmarried and with no girlfriend, no ambition and no goals is now prevalent in our culture. This same young man is frequently pictured as lacking, in addition to the other markers of adulthood, financial and emotional independence since he still lives with his parents, probably in the basement.

This is a frivolous man. He is frivolous because he is disconnected from the depths of life, from the thoughts and behaviors that would move him to full and mature adulthood. Devoted to maintaining a child-like existence in which he takes no responsibility, he engages life in only the most superficial ways with no focus, no intensity, and no burning desire to contribute to family, neighbor or friend.

On the other end of the spectrum, we have the hard-charging, high-achiever. These people, while appearing to have a serious purpose, often do not. It is entirely possible to live a high-intensity life and remain frivolous.

Frivolousness

When our goals are not aligned with values deeper than merely optimizing our purchasing power, we remain fixed in a state of frivolousness.

While frivolousness can be easily spotted at the extremes, most of us do not inhabit the extremes. Most of us experience frivolousness in the middle. The men at that homeschool meeting with their silly hats represent this middling type.

Frivolousness, because it is the disconnection from mature life, can make itself seen and felt in many subtle ways, but what is common to them all is a basis in fear. Underlying all forms of frivolousness is the fear that we are not enough to face the seriousness of life straight on or that others will cut us down if they perceive us as taking ourselves and our tasks seriously.

In an entertainment-driven culture, we have many escape paths from seriousness. We can go our entire lives and never have to face the seriousness of life or confront our own unseriousness. The level of distraction we now face is unprecedented and so is our level of unseriousness.

The problems we face in life can often feel overwhelming. This is especially true in an atomized, individualistic culture where the governing axiom is "every man for himself!" When the supporting institutions of community, family and religion have been removed the individual is obligated to face the problems of life alone.

While these supporting institutions have been removed from most of our lives, the problems we deal with are more complicated than ever. As government and corporations have made inroads into every area of life, the bureaucratic difficulties we must wade through have become ever more arcane. Add to this the perennial human problems of supporting oneself: creating a meaningful life and happy relationships, and it is no wonder so many of feel at least some sense of inadequacy as we contemplate these challenges.

It is easier to retreat from them as far as possible into frivolousness. The retreat of many adults, for example, into meaningless "fandoms" is a mark of this. Adults who spend time and money indulging in fantasy play, dressing up as comic book characters and collecting expensive toys related to some media project directed at a juvenile audience embody a now rampant form of frivolousness. Rather than working within the confines of reality to create a life that is both serious and meaningful, these people simply retreat, looking for meaning through identification with a corporate product created by others.

Disappearance into passing pleasures is also a mark of running from the seriousness of life, of fleeing the serious consequences of our choices by attempting to make no important decisions. When your biggest decision is which video game to play, your chances of facing serious outcomes are minimal.

At the same time, we see people retreating into other forms of frivolousness in an attempt to avoid pursuing serious purposes. To embrace and pursue a serious purpose in life is necessarily to put oneself into positions that demand growth. Growth demands effort, risk and change. People resist these because the initial stages involve unpleasant sensations whether that is the feeling of muscles tensing with exertion at the gym or the feeling of nervousness in the belly just prior to speaking up in public. When we give into the temptation to avoid these negative feelings, we surrender the opportunity to grow.

The Consequences of Avoiding the Serious

If we make a habit of avoiding all initially negative sensations, we eventually find we are avoiding the serious purposes life has called us to pursue. We find we have not built the family we wanted, created the businesses we had in mind, taken the trips we desired. We find ourselves empty, lost and despairing, confused about what we should be doing and why.

Avoiding serious purposes has a cascading effect. Avoidance obscures our sense of what we should be doing. Each choice is like a leaf in autumn falling across a sign placed on the ground that points us toward the right road. One leaf won't change anything, but enough leaves together can block our vision totally. This is how our decisions to avoid the pains growth requires work: one alone isn't that big a deal, but too many cause us to lose sight of what we are meant to go.

Losing sight of our purpose hurts, and it is not the good, profitable pain of growth, but the pain of atrophy, decay and death. Most of us continue our pattern of avoiding pain in this situation, in fact, many kick it into hyperdrive as we seek to lose ourselves in frivolousness to avoid the pain our previous avoidances have caused.

Sometimes, people escape into frivolousness because they fear others' opinions. Our culture has come to regard seriousness as the enemy of joy and authenticity. The second-worst kind of people, we are taught, are those who take ideas seriously, people who allow their convictions to interfere with their duties to consume and to conform. The worst kind of people, our society tells us, are those who take not only their ideas seriously, but themselves as well.

Frivolousness

Taking oneself seriously is an offense against the egalitarian spirit. One who takes himself and his endeavors seriously implies that he and his aims are important, at least to himself, and therefore, he seems to imply he believes himself to be more important than others. Thus the frivolousness people adopt to avoid being seen by others as proud also roots itself in fear: fear of being disliked, fear of being cut down.

The only way out of this situation is to cultivate courage. Facing the seriousness of our choices, purposes and relationships requires an uncommon amount of it. Most people lack courage and the constant companion of cowardice is frivolousness.

Fortunately, it works the other way too. The more seriously we take our choices, purposes and selves, the more we will find that we are able to face bravely the challenges the pursuit of these ends forces upon us.

To grow serious requires, like all growth in virtue, training ourselves to choose what is good. Needless to say, taking the Good seriously is a prerequisite to learning to choose it habitually.

This need not be a morose process. Growth in virtue and maturity can be a source of great happiness. Virtue frees us from the shackles of our self-imposed spiritual prisons, and that liberation is cause for rejoicing. As we begin to renounce frivolousness, we will find that behind the seriousness we must pursue lurks not misery, but maturity and deep joy. And joy, we know, is the most serious thing there is.

5

Sloth

Encountering Sloth

I DIDN'T WANT TO write this chapter. There were less demanding things to do. I have Netflix, and there are literally thousands of hours of television I have not watched. The recliner in the living room is pretty comfortable too. It would be easy to while away my time in this way. Many people do.

The temptation to avoid work and make ease our top priority is the temptation to sloth. Some instances of sloth, like the one I just mentioned, are obvious: sitting in a chair escaping into entertainment rather than doing the hard work of life. Other examples may be less obvious.

Sloth can be physical, as in the example above, or it can be mental and spiritual. Even a man who works hard all day in a physically demanding job can be slothful if he refuses to develop his intellect and personality. This may not seem like a big deal. Who cares if we slouch a little in one area if other parts of our lives stay afloat?

To answer this requires some context. The damaging effects of sloth cannot be understood apart from an understanding of human purpose and the role of work in achieving that purpose. We must begin with the assumption that each of us has within us latent gifts, talents and abilities. When brought to full flower, these qualities produce good outcomes for ourselves and others. The trouble is that the process of bringing these from their inchoate potential to full maturity is not easy.

It is not easy because much in the world opposes this process. We are surrounded by temptations, by distractions both internal and external.

Nevertheless, life demands we not be slothful because of what Stephen Pressfield has called Resistance[1]. Resistance is the part of reality that pushes back. Resistance resists. When we set our minds to changing some bad habit or to cultivating some new good habit, Resistance resists. When we try to improve a relationship, Resistance rears its head. Resistance threatens all our noble intentions and fancy aspirations. It seeks to undermine our courage and invites us as seductively as possible to give up.

Resistance opposes all our efforts to bring our unique blends of gifts and talents to fruition. This is not entirely bad news. We need this resistance because the resistance causes our talents to grow. Just like a weightlifter's muscles only enlarge when they strain against the iron, so all our more invisible gifts only grow when they push against the resistance they encounter.

Anyone who has ever tried to pick up a form of artistic expression or to learn a musical instrument knows this. Imagine a woman who, in middle age, decides to take up painting. Her mind is full of beautiful portraits and landscapes she hopes to capture. But when she touches her brush to the canvas, what comes out doesn't resemble her mental image in the slightest.

She cannot express her vision because her skills are not developed. Between what she can conceive with her mind and what she can create with her hands lies a chasm. Labor is the only available bridge. Only by repeated practice applying the paint to canvas will her abilities grow. Only through observation and study will the image in her mind finally express itself as art.

This is how life is. The gap between what we want to do, to be, to have and where we are at the moment is always significant. Because overcoming this gap requires work, sloth is serious. Sloth causes us to shrink back from doing the work required to become what we could. Whatever in us resists the painful process of going from someone who merely wants to be an artist, a race car driver, a doctor, a mother or any myriad of other things to being a person who actually is those things is sloth.

The Costs of Sloth

Because sloth prevents us from being all that we are capable of being, giving into it erodes our dignity. Give in enough, and giving in becomes a habit. Habitually choosing sloth stymies our development. Any creature whose development is stymied doesn't stay in neutral. It stalls and eventually decays.

1. Pressfield, *The War of Art*, 4

This is a critical truth: sloth doesn't merely stop us from moving forward, it sends us backward. This is easy to see when we think about finances. The Bible puts it this way: "A little sleep, a little slumber, a little folding of the hands to rest, and poverty will come upon you like a robber, and want like an armed man. [2]

Obviously, the author of this proverb is not arguing we should never sleep. He is making the point that repeatedly choosing rest over work always leads to negative consequences. Particularly worth noting is that sloth brings poverty. Poverty is not a homeostatic state. It is not a state where all things are working well together to maintain a status quo. Sloth, he is pointing out, does not mean that expenses perfectly match income every month for a total change of zero dollars. No, he is pointing out that sloth actually leads to need, to being at less than zero, living in the negative. Sloth creates a hole you have to dig out of. In the end, avoiding the work we should have done in the moment creates a greater burden that must eventually be shouldered.

A life of sloth is one not lived in the full light of truth. The idea that shirking labor does not cause us to slide backward is one of the delusions on which sloth depends. No one who lives a truthful life can deny the necessity of work. Another delusion to which the slothful succumb is that work is an inherent evil. The slothful believe work should be avoided when possible and minimized when it can't.

This delusion mischaracterizes the nature of work. Some work, yes, is onerous. It may be difficult, may be very demanding. This is especially true of work that demands great physical exertion. When we push our bodies to, or sometimes even past, the limits of what they can do, we pay a price. We can become exhausted or injured.

But even physically demanding work is not a curse. It tires us, but enough of it done within reasonable limits, strengthens us too. Physical work increases our physical capacity. Manual, physical labor offers unique satisfactions. Physical work brings about physical results. When we have finished a job of this sort, we are left with results we can see. When we undertake to build a wall or install a garden, we can stand back to see that at the end of the day a wall or garden exists that once did not. This sense of being able to bring into being something that did not previously exist is one of the rewards the slothful deny themselves.

Because they avoid work, the slothful also avoid the rewards of work. This is how their delusions survive. Positive rewards from working would

2. Prov 24: 33–34 ESV

challenge the belief that work is inherently bad. If work were seen as the pathway to desired goods, the slothful's delusion would shatter because work would have to be seen in a more balanced, nuanced light. Rather than maintain that work is inherently bad, the slothful man would be forced to see that work is, at least, a mixed bag, a sometimes exhausting, demanding endeavor that can yield great rewards.

The Roots of Sloth

In the slothful man's case, it is entirely possible that somewhere in his experience, the connection between work and reward was broken. This can happen easily when we are young. This connection can break if we find ourselves in a situation where we work hard to earn a reward and then find that reward denied to us. If we are promised, say, an ice cream cone after we finish some chore and our parent forgets to provide it, the connection between work and reward may be broken. If this happens repeatedly or even if the link between work and reward is intermittent, our trust in the process will be diminished.

When this link is diminished or broken in childhood, it becomes easier to live a life of sloth as an adult. All work involves an element of faith. We must trust that our labor is not in vain. If, because of our prior experience, we no longer trust that the process of work and reward will hold for us, our motivation to work will be lower. If it is low enough, we find ourselves lost in sloth.

It is also easy to fall into the delusion that work is something to be done merely for pay. This delusion flourishes in a society where employment by others is the norm. In agricultural societies and societies where many people were apprenticed into trades and made their livings independent from employers, it might have been easier to see the way that increased work, risk taking, and innovation led directly to increased prosperity. In an economy like that, it may have been clearer that a willingness to do more than the minimum contributes to our wellbeing.

In an economy where we have all largely traded the freedom of independent work for the security of regular employment, this is harder to see. We go to work, clock in and know that most of what we do on any given day will have no effect on the size of our paycheck at the end of the week. The guaranteed reward motivates us to do less than we might if the entirety of our income depended on what we do each moment of the day.

The average American worker has little impetus to go beyond his prescribed duties, because his paychecks roll in with predictable regularity. While this is not necessarily sloth, the atrophy of the soul which it induces is similar.

When we do no more work than the minimum required to earn a paycheck, we suffer. We may suffer financially and professionally, but we will also suffer spiritually. This is because, contrary to the delusion that work is an inherent evil, work is a positive good.

Understanding the Blessing of Work

Sloth is a fundamental disconnection from the goodness of work. The slothful need to grasp that work is a good because it bridges the gap between what we are and what we can be, because it inspires our self-respect, and because it helps us to actualize and express our natures as creative beings. Human beings were meant to create, to bring into being what before had no being.

When we succumb to the temptation to sloth, we surrender our hold on this essential part of our nature. Unlike all other creatures, human beings have the capacity for long-term planning, for art, for engineering. We are uniquely endowed with the capacity to imagine what we have not seen and to make it visible.

We do this, of course, on scales both small and large. On the micro level, we can make a daily list of next steps toward realizing some vision in our minds. Perhaps that vision entails a mown lawn, a healthy meal, a completed work task. When we work at these things, we are not merely engaging in meaningless drudgery, but exercising a power something like God's: the power to bring new realities into being.

Unlike God, we cannot bring them into being merely by speaking. We must act. A slothful refusal to acting not only deprives us of the external rewards that would accrue to us through our labor, but also robs us of the ability to manifest this God-like aspect of our nature. When we refuse to exercise this part of ourselves, we grow weaker. When we shrink from the work required to bring new realities into being, we shrink from ourselves, reject our natures, and turn ourselves into creatures less than we would otherwise be.

Before we look at what the slothful person can do to become less slothful, we should consider one more dynamic that may lie behind the adoption of slothful habits. Exploring the dynamics of sloth is important because behavior is always motivated. We have reasons for what we do or, in the case of slothfulness, what we don't do. Without understanding more than the surface of sloth, we might miss what's really important.

The real concern about slothfulness is that in its atrophying of the human will, it leads to dependency. Infants are dependent. Little children are dependent. The process of maturation is the process of first becoming independent and then moving toward interdependence, the ability to work with others to achieve a goal. When we achieve interdependence we can not only take care of ourselves, but are able to work together with others to form complex, beneficial relationships.

When we succumb to sloth, we short-circuit this process. Though we grow physically, we remain in an infantile state emotionally, psychologically and spiritually. One of the great blessings of work is that through encountering its struggles and challenges, we move out of our childishness.

Children, of course, are a blessing. Adults who remain children are not. By refusing to engage the challenges of a working life, these childish adults become a burden, forcing others to make up for their lack of ability to provide for themselves or to handle the challenges of life. They force others to do not only their own work, but additional work that rightly belongs to the slothful person.

The slothful man then is always in a state of insecurity because his welfare depends upon the charity of others. When others decide not to continue their habit of supporting him, his fortunes will suffer. The slothful man knows this and worry sets in. Too often instead of turning to work in his worry, he simply redoubles his habits of sloth, seeking to forget.

One reason he may have become slothful in the first place is that his options for work may all be unappealing. This is not unreasonable. The specialization of the modern world creates things, places, and institutions normal people find hard to care about. The emptiness of so much modern work occasions something that looks like sloth, but may actually be apathy.

Instead of rushing to judgement, let's take a moment and consider the context. For millions of people, work is separated from any tangible or visible product. Most see little effect from their work. Few, at the end of the day, leave work able to see some product or even a change brought about by their efforts. When work is a day-in-day-out proposition that leaves little to show for it, apathy is a reasonable response.

Consider too how many people are employed by agencies and corporations whose very purpose is trivial: making more widgets, selling more widgets. I am reminded of the videos available online of gatherings of employees at some big-box megastore being led in cheers prior to opening on a big sales day. The false enthusiasm in these videos is pathetic. Everyone from the manager leading the cheer down to the lowliest employee is faking it. The inauthenticity is palpable. No employee would choose to be at work if he could be anywhere else. The inward cringing of the leader is almost visible as he works to rouse people to the requisite level of cheer.

Nobody on screen really cares. Behind all the mandatory cheer is an apathy that orients people toward watching the clock, counting the minutes until the shift is over, and doing just enough to get by in the meantime. In situations like this, we can understand the apathy. What normal person would be inspired by pretending to love putting another pair of cheap sneakers on a shelf, unloading yet another truck full of cheap electronics, or putting away disposable clothes?

These are just a few scenarios where apathy can lead to sloth. To escape sloth requires a connection to meaningful and authentic labor. Both of these things are largely denied to modern workers. Without them, apathy sets in, and if we do not do the work necessary to overcome it, the apathy will lead to sloth..

Escaping Sloth

What then is the man or woman caught in the snare of sloth supposed to do? No one accustomed to a slothful existence is likely to get to work without a process of reformation. This makes sloth a particularly difficult vice to escape. Getting free from any vice requires work and, as we have established, work is precisely what the slothful avoid.

So, to begin, the slothful man must acknowledge his problem. He must see what his disconnection from meaningful work is costing him and those close to him. He must see that his habits endanger him and his future financially, that his sloth prevents him from taking full advantage of the opportunities life presents him, and that it stymies his growth. At first, he may have only a hint of this truth. The important thing at this stage is not to suppress what knowledge one does have.

Normally, this knowledge first presents itself as a nagging feeling that something isn't as it should be. The slothful one may find herself subject to intense bouts of anxiety. This is a sign that she has failed to attend to problems that need attention. Perhaps, too, her physical surroundings will be speak. A pile of unwashed dishes, a failure to leave the house for multiple consecutive days, a generally messy atmosphere, all these say that one has succumbed to sloth. Developing the requisite sensitivity to the meaning of these signs and a willingness to respond positively to them is the way forward.

Next, the slothful man must survey his life to determine how his slothful habits have made themselves known. Perhaps he has a history of problems at work, perhaps unpaid bills, perhaps a pattern of disrupted relationships. All these and more are born of sloth.

Once this survey is complete, a plan for change is necessary. Whatever this plan is, start slow. Sloth, like all vices, has both bodily and spiritual aspects. Any change will require addressing both of these aspects. Sloth makes us weaker in both these areas. The physical weakness will likely be the first focus. To get up off the couch and start working will be uncomfortable. It might actually hurt.

He must stick with it. Above all, slothfulness is a failure of perseverance. Sloth undertakes projects up to the point where they become difficult and then surrenders. The difference between the slothful person and the productive one is that the productive person endures the difficulty inherent in bringing any project to completion.

If difficulty were not inherent in every project we undertake, sloth would not be a vice. If creating value and bringing new realities into being were easy, perseverance would not be a virtue. As it is, perseverance is a virtue because it is the opposite of sloth. Rather than simply giving up when he hits resistance, the non-slothful person presses on toward the goal.

Learning to do this will require a new level of awareness. Often we fall into slothful patterns because we do not pay enough attention to our own feelings and behavior. We easily convince ourselves to take a shortcut or to avoid some onerous task altogether without even knowing it. Only in retrospect do we see what we have done.

One good way to develop this new level of awareness is to think deeply about what we are aiming at. A goal we believe in is a good motivator, but it also gives us something by which we can measure our progress. When we can look objectively at whether or not we are progressing toward our goal, we can see the measure of our sloth. If we are closer to the goal than we were in the recent past, we can be assured that we have been less slothful.

At the same time, fixing our minds on a goal, returning regularly to our mental image of it can help us to develop greater awareness of where we are shirking the tasks required to achieve it. When we look at our feelings and behaviors in light of a goal, especially a goal delayed or unfulfilled, that light exposes our slothfulness. Though this exposure might be painful, if we take seriously what it reveals we will begin to see the justifications, even the unconscious ones, we have used to excuse our taking it easy rather than moving forward.

Seeing these truths helps us to integrate a new level of awareness about ourselves, and we can use this new level of awareness to overcome our slothful inclinations. When we notice that we are avoiding work, we can see the ways we are undermining our plans and, with a little effort, stop.

Of course, awareness doesn't guarantee permanent change. We must remain vigilant. Falling back into slothful patterns is easy, and things that are easy are more likely to be done than things that are difficult. The temptation to abandon our work will always be there.

But to return to the point made at the beginning of this chapter, we work because it is the key to our growth. Sloth stymies the growth plan inside of us. It prevents us from doing the work on which the emergence of our fullest selves depends. When we accept this, we can see that work is not always an onerous duty placed upon us from the outside. Rather, work can be a joy when we pursue it as the means by which we are transformed from our nascent, caterpillar selves to our mature butterfly selves.

When this is our attitude, work becomes a central part of a rewarding life. We have the opportunity to go about our work meditatively. We have the opportunity to observe the process rather than to focus merely on results. We get to observe the process not just of the work we produce, but of the way the work produces us.

Above all, we can come to understand our work as an extension of ourselves. The more we commit to work and to Insert "to"reject sloth, the bigger and more expansive our souls and worlds become. We offer our work to the world for the elevation of our fellows and finally see that in doing so, we lift ourselves toward our destiny.

6

Unforgiveness

The Sorcery of Unforgiveness

WHEN WE ARE HURT, we naturally desire something that will protect us from ever hurting again. We long for armor that might allow us to walk through the world impervious to its many pains and difficulties. This is especially true when those pains and difficulties come through the choices of other people. When others hurt us, we may avoid them or we may strike back.

Because walking through the world in external, physical armor is impractical, we develop an inner, emotional armor. We cling to our resentments, transforming them from soft wounds into hard scars. We wear them as a shield over our vulnerable places. This may seem a reasonable approach given what we have experienced. The problem is that if we wear it long enough, our armor of scars becomes part of us, and we find ourselves unable to move easily. What was intended to protect now weighs us down. Instead of becoming free, we find we have ossified and become immobile. This is the sorcery of unforgiveness. It turns us from pliable and flexible creatures into those incapable of real movement.

Obviously, this is a metaphor. Unforgiveness doesn't literally turn us to stone, doesn't literally morph our skin into steel. What it actually does is restrict our inner world. As we harbor unforgiveness, we lose our inner freedom. Unforgiveness hinders our growth and traps us in repetitive and often destructive patterns. In short, unforgiveness prevents us from becoming all we were intended to be, and shapes us instead into a false version of ourselves, a parody of the person we could be. Rather than inhabiting the world as our freest and best selves, we become uncanny, like a doll or statue bearing only a faint resemblance to what we really are.

The Unforgiveness Disconnection

The trouble is that there is just so much to forgive. The experience of being mistreated, hurt, abused or otherwise injured by another is universal. We all go through it. We all hurt others as well. This is so inherent in our human experience that even to say it seems unnecessary, redundant. As we experience more and more of these hurts, without a means of forgiving them, we find ourselves increasingly disconnected from others. Only by escaping the bonds of our unforgiveness can we find remedy.

Our first step toward living free from the imprisoning power of unforgiveness is to take stock of how often in life we experience the pain that makes it necessary. Think back to your early life. Start with your earliest memory and move forward in time. Review your memories in this way and it won't be long before you find something to forgive, some memory that causes you to wince when recalling it. For some of us, our very first memory is traumatic. From the get go, we were burdened with some terrible grievance to forgive.

Repeat this exercise but from the other side. This time go through your memories and look at all the times you have, even inadvertently, caused pain or suffering for others. My guess is that you won't get far this time either before you come across some memory that causes you to cringe and wish you had made another choice.

The point of these exercises is not to inflict pain. I am not asking you to engage in some masochistic ritual whose only purpose is to hurt you. I merely want to make you aware of how much forgiveness and its opposite are woven into the basic fabric of our experience. Escaping the decision to forgive or to harbor unforgiveness is as impossible as escaping the hurtful experiences that make it necessary.

Life demands we forgive daily. Most people don't, at least not as deeply or as fully as is necessary to truly lay down the resentments they carry. Some people don't forgive at all and instead become more and more trapped in their anger and resentment. These people eventually cease to function fully. Their disconnection metastasizes to all areas of life.

Unforgiveness

The Varieties of Unforgiveness and Malignant Anger

Let's turn first to the more run of the mill unforgiveness, and the problems that typically attend it. Ordinary unforgivenesses express themselves in many ways. We can categorize them as those ways that affect the self internally and those that affect relationships with others.

Carrying around ongoing unforgiveness shapes our identity. People who cling to their pain become certain sorts of people. Unforgiveness infuses our personalities with anger. When we hold onto our grievances against others, we take what might once have been a justified response to a damaging or unfair situation, and turn it into a pervasive personality trait. This anger then expresses itself in times and places far removed from the original offense.

A word about anger is warranted here. Unless we grasp its legitimate function, we won't know how to put it to its right use. Anger is a good gift and helps us to preserve both our lives and inner selves when used rightly. Anger gives us energy for breaking negative bonds and for stopping aggression. This is easy to see in the physical realm. Imagine a woman alone at night who is suddenly accosted by an attacker. He wraps his arms around her tightly and whispers threatening words. We would all agree that anger on her part would be right and proper. Her anger would power her to break the bonds of her assailant's grip, to do her utmost to stop his unprovoked aggression. In this way, her anger would serve her well.

When we transfer this concept out of the purely physical realm to the realm of relationships and emotions, we can see that the same principles apply. At some point in our lives, we all experience relational and verbal aggression from another. It is our healthy anger that energizes us to demand that such behavior stop. It is our healthy anger that might lead us to break the bonds that tie us to a person who will not stop. These situations tend to be more subtle and complex than being jumped in the dark by some malicious stranger. Even so, our anger is right and healthy and good when it serves to energize us to keep ourselves safe and whole.

Though anger can serve a healthy purpose, that purpose can be perverted in a couple of ways. First, we might feel anger as the energy to protect ourselves, but not be able to act on our own behalf. Second, we might cling to our anger long after the threat has passed. The two are related as we shall see.

First, many of us have experienced violations of our person or will while we were vulnerable or under someone else's power. We felt the energy anger gave us to protect ourselves, but were, for some reason, unable to take the action was necessary to secure our safety. The resultant mix of emotional and physical damage is called trauma.

This might have happened to us when we were children, when we were at school, when we were in the military or in any situation where our power to flee was compromised or our ability to fight back reduced. I experienced these situations often at school. The power differential between students and teachers is extreme. Consider the fact that teachers can leave a situation with a student whenever they like, but that students are prevented by law and custom from leaving school without authorization. Every instance of bullying by a teacher or administrator, every time a teacher yells or makes a cutting remark can become an occasion for trauma. Some people experience similar dynamics even when they are at their most vulnerable, ever in their closest familial relationships.

These experiences fill us with anger, with the energy to protect ourselves, but since we cannot act in the interest of self preservation, we cannot discharge that energy rightly. At that point, we may do a couple of things with it. We may turn it inward and become self-abusive, or we may simply hold it, letting it linger in our minds and personalities until we forget its origins and its presence begins to feel normal.

Both of these paths shape our self-understanding, our identity. We may become self-loathing. We may, at a barely conscious level, try to explain the trauma we experienced by telling ourselves we deserved it. If we could not escape what was done to us, we think, perhaps we can at least make it intelligible by concluding that the behavior that so damaged us was justified by our badness.

Telling ourselves that we deserved whatever was done to us has one huge drawback: it isn't true. Rather than allowing us to have a reliable and objective self-understanding a choice to turn our healthy anger inward and away from those whose violations inspired it skews our self-understanding.

A skewed self-understanding inevitably leads to poor choices. These poor choices only create more damage and injury to our already weakened sense of self. A pattern of turning once healthy anger on ourselves means the abuse never stops. The only difference is that we carry on where our original abuser left off.

Some people attempt to hold the anger static in their souls rather than turning it fully on themselves. In this case, rather than becoming people who are shy, self-deprecating, reserved and self-loathing, they become hard, suspicious, indifferent and anxious. This happens when we have a sense that whatever trauma we suffered was wrong, and we know that we were not to blame. When we hold our anger static, we neither release it, nor direct it. Rather, we simply let it sit.

In this case, our anger becomes a cry for justice. We look at what we have suffered and lost, and we see nothing has been done to balance the scales. Not only are we forced to live with the memory of the offense, we must live with the fact that the offender got away with it. One way of coping is to direct the anger not like a laser pointed at ourselves but like a floodlight at everyone.

This can be a subtle move. People who've chosen this path don't lash out at everyone. It's not that they can't have friends, but that they wear their anger like protective gear, a shell designed to prevent their ever being taken in again. These people may think of themselves as skeptical, as hard-edged, as tough. People who choose this path sometimes imagine others can't see that they live behind their shield. But others do see. When we make anger part of our identity, it's obvious. So is the hurt underneath.

People seek to establish relationships with others they perceive as being similar to themselves. As a result of projecting a "tough" image, people tend to draw into their lives other people just as angry and full of unforgiveness as themselves. This has a compounding effect. Two or more angry people in relationship eventually leads to additional offenses. In groups like this, drama never ends. The result is yet more pain and damage that will either have to be forgiven or held onto endlessly. For those who choose to retain their anger, the armor becomes ever thicker, their view of the world ever darker, and the people they draw to themselves ever more dysfunctional. In this way, a refusal to forgive can initiate a downward spiral that ends in death, if not a physical death, then a spiritual one.

Whether we direct our anger toward ourselves or try to keep it alive by holding it static, anger narrows our attention. Anger and unforgiveness shape our vision of reality so that we see only what reinforces our sense of violation, our feeling of victimhood. The world comes to seem ever more dangerous. Whatever we see or experience reinforces an identity which has its roots in some long-ago offense and which we have nurtured across time through their choices.

This narrowed vision and the ongoing pain of carrying anger over past offenses inevitably creates problems in relationships. Both of these sorts of people may lash out angrily at others. Because they carry so much anger from past experiences, they often have what is called "a temper". This temper is really an inability to handle new and frustrating situations appropriately. A load of anger from the past means anger in the present becomes hard to regulate.

People who can't regulate their anger will always have turbulent relationships. By pumping anger into every situation people who have not let go of past offenses recreate the chaos of their past. Life becomes an endless loop of similar scenarios. Rather than making progress, many people feel compelled to create further trauma. Thus does their anger keep them from moving forward. As these people live and relive traumatic scenarios, their narrowed focus is justified in their minds. "See," they seem to think, "this is what all people are like. I'm justified in my self-hatred and suspicion. This always happens to me." What their narrowed attentions cannot admit is the possibility that their commitment to unforgiveness shapes their experience.

Escaping the Unforgiveness Pattern

The only way out of this situation is to forgive. Hurt and traumatized people might balk at hearing this, but it's true. Only by releasing the anger over what was done to us can we experience new situations for what they are rather than as reflections of events long ago. People resist forgiving for several reasons. If letting go is ever to be a possibility, we will have to look at the reasons we may be reluctant to do so.

First, for those who have allowed anger and unforgiveness to become part of their identity, letting go means a deep change in how they understand themselves. Changing our vision of ourselves is hard. Changing the basic way we see and interpret the world is hard. Changing the tone of our interactions with others is hard. Increasing our awareness of ourselves and our reactions to stimuli is hard. And yet, releasing anger and moving toward forgiveness requires all these.

To make these things a bit easier, we should understand forgiveness as a process, not as a single "over and done" action. I have said that the problem with unforgiveness is that it stagnates our growth, and growth is the operative word to remember here.

Rather than expecting forgiveness to happen in an instant, we should think of it as an expression of maturity we are aiming toward. An ability to forgive is a sign that we are inhabiting our personality in full. When we forgive, who we are is no longer constricted by the anger we feel over past offenses. Those bonds have fallen away. Until we are moving toward forgiveness, we will never fully be the person we were intended to become.

Just as any organism does not grow to full maturity in an instant, but rather through a largely imperceptible process, so do we grow when we decide to release our unforgiveness. What matters is not whether we forgive perfectly or even quickly, what matters is that we recognize that our best selves, the fullness of what we were meant to be, lies in the direction of forgiving, and that we cease to justify our unforgiveness and begin to relax our grip on it.

This is difficult because deep down we feel a need for justice. In many ways, our struggle with unforgiveness is our struggle with the fact that the world is less than perfectly just, that people can mistreat others, can mistreat us, and get away with it. Rather than accepting this truth and the vulnerability it can make us feel, we cling to our resentment as a means of trying to balance the scales.

This line of thinking is not entirely wrong. The diagnosis is right, but the prescription for cure faulty. When we are mistreated and offended against, a desire for justice is perfectly reasonable. We want some authority to pronounce judgement against the offender and to proclaim our innocence. We want to be understood and to be compensated for the losses we have incurred.

Forgiveness means accepting that this kind of justice will not be coming. In order to release our unforgiveness we must accept that while our desire for justice is real and may be justified, such justice rarely comes. Even if the person who hurt us was held accountable for his actions and punished, he would never be able to undo the original offense. No matter what, things cannot be put back the way they were before the damaging event.

The hope implicit in forgiveness is that in the long run, things will in some ways be better than they were before, that we will have grown past the anger and incorporated the damages we suffered into a healthier personality characterized by inner freedom.

Clinging to our demands for justice is the opposite of inner freedom. We delude ourselves into thinking that somehow our refusal to let go of our demands for justice will change anything We imagine that clinging to our demands for justice will cause someone, somewhere to bring it about. It won't.

People make their demands for justice a central part of their personality because they hope that since justice has not come, others will at least see that we have been victimized. They hope a scowl and a tough attitude will alert people to their hurt. If we cannot have justice for the offender, we hope at least to have pity for ourselves. This is another reason why surrendering our unforgiveness is difficult: because through holding onto it, we can retain our identity as victim and, we hope, a life where others refrain from injuring us further out of pity.

Others' pity will, we hope, cause them to go easy on us, to lower their expectations. We hope others will see our damaged state and compensate our losses by being particularly thoughtful or considerate of us. We hope to escape the burden of our own responsibilities by telegraphing weakness in the hopes others will shoulder what is ours to carry.

As much as forgiveness means freedom for us, it also means owning up to the responsibility inherent in being a choice-making human being. In order to surrender our unforgiveness, we must be willing to give up both our demands for justice and our attempts to avoid full adult responsibility. Both the ability to give up demands for justice and the acceptance of responsibility are characteristics of the mature human being.

And that is the goal. We cannot achieve maturity except through expiating the things that are blocking it. If you are a person who is carrying a significant amount of unforgiveness, then your road to full maturity is blocked. To move forward, you must clear the path. But, you say, how do I do that?

The first step is to unclench one's inner fists. This means moving away from viewing forgiveness as an abstraction or as an excuse. Many people see forgiveness as an ideal only. They imagine that forgiveness is a nice sentiment that is somehow irrelevant to them and their situations. Perhaps, we imagine that forgiveness is for when a stranger in a parking lot inadvertently scratches our car, or someone cuts in front of us in line. We do not imagine it is for the serious stuff. Forgiveness matters most for the serious stuff. The most damaging experiences require forgiveness most urgently.

Unclenching one's fists means moving from believing that forgiveness is not for us to believing that forgiveness is a necessity for everyone. We must move from not wanting to forgive to desiring to do so. We must give up the idea that to forgive someone is to excuse their behavior, to somehow say or signal that their violations we suffered were really ok. Too many of us seem to imagine that if we forgive something, then what we forgave must not have been that big a deal to begin with. But this idea arises from our damaged selves and is not true.

Unforgiveness

Once you have moved from being suspicious of forgiveness to trusting its efficacy, we can begin to take important steps. The first one is to accept that you are commencing a journey toward forgiveness, not forgiving in an instant. You must understand that forgiveness is both a decision and a practice. It involves deciding not to allow some violation you experienced define who you are, and practicing changing the way you think and feel when you regard past harms.

Forgiveness requires taking responsibility. It requires us to pursue positive goals and to hold ourselves accountable for pursuing them rather than merely living in reaction to what happened to us. It means regarding past harms as an obstacle to our achieving all we feel called to achieve. It means beginning to regard ourselves as overcomers, not as victims merely.

Forgiveness means taking stock of our mortality as well. We must remember that both we and the person who hurt us will die. What happened to us will eventually be lost to history. The trouble with unforgiveness is that it lures us toward living a life focused on defense instead of contribution and and a life that makes no contribution will itself be utterly lost to history. Unforgiveness threatens not merely our hearts, but our legacies.

Forgiving is not a balanced process. While forgiveness demands action and change on our part, it demands nothing on the part of the one we are forgiving. We need not even tell the object of our forgiveness that we are forgiving him. Forgiveness can be done alone, in secret. We do not need the other person to admit his need for forgiveness. We do not need his consent or cooperation. We do not need him to change.

The unilateral nature of forgiveness is part of the freedom it offers us. We act as we desire, regardless of the behavior of the other. In forgiveness, we declare independence from others who have wronged us. We take an action they cannot control. We forgive because we desire freedom and growth and our own well-being. If the violations we experienced were an enslaving of our souls, by moving toward forgiveness, we emancipate them, set them free, not for the sake of the other, but for our own sake and for the sake of the good a free soul brings into the world.

7

Covetousness

Our Troubled Relationship with Desire

DESIRING IS AT THE heart of being human. Often this desiring bears profitable fruit. Without the human capacity for desire, we'd be lost. All the accrued blessings of history, from great works of art and architecture to the most advanced medicines, had their beginnings in a desiring mind. When functioning in its positive role, desire drives us to reach our creative potential and thus to bequeath to posterity gifts that enhance life for generations.

The problem with desires is that they require labor to fulfill. We can want and want and want and, without doing the necessary work, those wants will never be satisfied. Desires necessarily remain thoughts, abstract ideas about what we would like to have or experience, if we do not take action to make them real.

All actions which might make real the objects of our desire have a cost. Even if that cost is merely being tired at the end of the day, it must be paid. When we consistently pay these costs, which can range from simply the inconvenience of running a necessary errand to footing the bill to start a business, we make investments in the actualization of our desires.

The natural temptation is to look for ways to achieve our desires without our paying the costs. We look for shortcuts. The problem with shortcuts is that they don't work. I am not talking here about legitimate improvements in efficiency that reduce costs, but about attempts to get around the idea of costs altogether. Those never work because they are an attempt to overthrow the structure of reality, of what simply is.

The worst kind of shortcut involves trying to take what another has earned. People who do this are thieves. At the bottom of all thievery is the desire to profit by stealing the results of another's labor.

Most of us aren't thieves. We don't go around taking from people the just rewards of their work. But thievery has an inner dynamic that we all experience. See, desire does not always function positively. When desire moves outside of the bounds where it can remain healthy and functional, it transforms into dangerous versions of itself. The desire to have something we have not earned or to prevent others from enjoying the just rewards of their choices is covetousness.

Covetousness and Desire

Covetousness is common, making at least a brief appearance in every human heart, and yet not widely understood. Perhaps one reason why is that it is an attitude that colors our perspectives rather than a single, discreet act or series of actions. Covetousness is often invisible. We can hide it. We can cling to it while we cover it with masks ranging from the repulsive to the comely. However we mask it, covetousness remains ugly. The right response to it, as to all vices, is not to mask it, but to renounce it. Without this renunciation, we remain forever alienated from true satisfaction. To be alienated from satisfaction is to doom ourselves to exhaustion. By attempting to gratify every petty desire, we sentence ourselves to a life in which we can never be satiated.

Before we talk about how this situation might be overcome, let's look at some of its more common expressions. Remember that covetousness is the desire to have without earning or to prevent another from enjoying the just rewards of his choices. When we see this vice described, we might initially think we would never indulge those sorts of sentiments.

But a second of reflection will reveal otherwise. The impulse to covet shows up in subtle ways. We see this more clearly when we apply this definition to instances where the object of the coveting is not material.

Common Covetousness in Context

Consider what happens when someone tries to rob another of the fruits of a good reputation. What might motivate someone to try to do this, to steal from another the hard-earned respect and trust of some mutual colleague or friend?

It begins with a judgment, of course. Behind all covetous behavior lies the determination that the person we are looking at simply does not deserve whatever reward they are enjoying. When we have made this judgment, justifying our covetous behavior becomes easier.

We convince ourselves that the other has attained his reward through illegitimate means. In the case of a good reputation, we might think that this person others so esteem became respected through putting up a false front, by pretending to be someone and something he is not. We begin to see him not as a person who has earned his good reputation through wise choices and treating others justly, but as master manipulator capable of fooling even the most insightful people around.

Once we convince ourselves of this person's deceptiveness, we see our attempts to destroy his reputation, to take away the earned results of his choices, as justified. We may convince ourselves that we are righting an injustice by exposing the truth. We might even imagine that by lowering others' estimation of our target, we are raising their estimation of us.

This is just one of the subtle ways covetousness works. Consider another example. When we try to take credit for another's professional achievementwe are coveting. This can happen between peers or between a subordinate and a supervisor. When someone takes unfair credit for what another has achieved, he allows his covetousness free reign.

In these situations, one person desires professional advancement and sees taking what rightly belongs to another as a shortcut to getting it. Such behavior, however, undermines the kind of real, sustainable and deserved trust on which all professional reputation is ultimately built.

Such things don't take place in just our professional lives, however. They can happen in our personal lives as well. The classic example is the coveting of a spouse or romantic partner. Though the context is different, the dynamics are the same. When we see a couple and determine that one member of that couple should be with us instead, and then act to make that happen, we are giving full reign to our covetousness.

Covetousness and Comparison

The point here is that though contexts change, the dynamics of covetousness remain the same. Regardless of the context in which it appears, covetousness is ultimately rooted in a comparison we make between ourselves and another. Typically, we come out on bottom in this comparison. Then, through a sophisticated mental operation, we move ourselves to the top.

Imagine this: a young man, let's call him Barney, has a romantic interest in a female friend. Somewhere along the course of their acquaintance, she begins dating another man, and that relationship grows more serious. Barney's anger and jealousy grow. He compares himself constantly to his love interest's boyfriend wondering what he has that Barney does not.

He knows the answer isn't nothing. He knows there must be some reason this young woman prefers her boyfriend to him, and so sets about mentally to discover what it is. Finally, he lands on something, some positive characteristic or quality that the boyfriend possesses that he lacks. Alternatively, he may identify in himself a negative trait he has that the boyfriend lacks. Whatever he settles on, he suspects this to be the reason she chose the other guy.

This assumption enflames his insecurities and makes him feel bad. Barney doesn't like to feel bad. He looks for a way out of this bad feeling. He finds it by reversing the question he's asking. No longer is he asking "what does he have that I don't?". He's now asking "What are that guy's flaws?" and "How could she fall for a guy like that?"

When he begins looking for the other guy's flaws, he finds plenty. Eventually, in his mind the other guy becomes such a monster that no actions against him are unjustified. When Barney reaches this point, he has given himself permission to act on his covetousness. At that point, he may resolve to do what he can to corrode his female friend's trust in her boyfriend in order to insinuate himself more fully into her affections.

Whether he succeeds or not depends on his level of skill. If he is skilled enough to work his corrupting magic subtly, he may succeed. If not, he'll likely fail. Either way, he has turned himself into a person whose covetousness and manipulativeness make him so untrustworthy that his chances of sustaining a happy relationship with anyone are slim.

Behind the Comparison Game

Still, we have not gotten to the bottom of the process. Something more is going on behind the scenes. At the very bottom, our man Barney has a problem even greater than his covetousness. His greater problem is the insecurity that leads him to lead a life of comparison with others. His covetousness springs from his inclination to look at others and compare them to himself, and this inclination stems from a search to reassure himself in the face of his insecurities.

It's important to note at the outset that Barney is operating on a delusion. He thinks he is comparing himself to others. What he is really doing is comparing his self-image to his mental image of others, to whom he imagines others to be. His entire life is rooted in an ongoing conflict of mirages. The constant comparisons of these false, one-dimensional images of himself and others drives him into a constant state of unrest.

When his self-image loses the comparison battle, he feels unworthy of the good things in his life. When his self-image wins the comparison battle, he feels entitled to more than he has and wonders why he has been cheated out of all that is owed. Either way, he loses.

Underneath this pattern lies his sense of insecurity, a lack of any serious sense of self-worth. Because his sense of self is not anchored in anything that tells him who he is, he must constantly look outward to see if he is "good enough" or whether others are "good enough". When he finds an imbalance between himself and others, he sets out to even the scores. This becomes the ground for his manipulative, undermining and controlling behavior.

If Barney's sense of self was more grounded, he would be more free from this cycle of comparison. If his understanding of himself were rooted in a mission he were trying to achieve or in a set of values he was trying to actualize, he could move through life without comparison. His only comparison would be of himself against his ideals. Daily, he could measure himself against his goals, looking at what progress he had made that day. His entire orientation would shift. No longer would his focus be on how he compares to others, but on how fully he is actualizing the values he holds dear.

Getting off the Comparison-Go-Round

Quitting the comparison game is the only way out of covetousness. The way out requires doing precisely what I have just described: anchoring oneself in something other than social comparison. To get off the comparison carousel Barney must look at what matters most to him. This requires an inward journey to discover his real values, and his mission and purpose in life. But that might hurt. It's much easier to stay hooked into the world of social comparison.

Covetousness

The social comparison habit is addictive because it offers immediate gratification. Using the word "gratification" here may sound strange knowing that at one level the comparison game makes us feel bad. But we can be gratified on many levels. What makes us feel bad on a surface level can make us feel good at a deeper level.

Let's go back to Barney. Barney finds gratification through the process of social comparison I have described. If he compares himself favorably to someone else, he feels more secure, and more proud of himself. He feels less vulnerable in the world. If he compares unfavorably, he finds gratification in the feeling of shame that comparison engenders.

This too might sound strange, but it's true. We all have had some experience of this. If we are honest, we know that bad feelings can offer their own sort of gratifications. We know that anger can make us feel powerful, that being made ashamed can make us feel excited, that being wronged often brings a rush of self-righteousness.

None of this means that the bad feelings don't actually feel bad, but that bad feelings bring us their own kind of stimulation and that stimulation has a gratifying effect. At one level, we know that feeling bad feels better to many people than the "nothing" they think they might feel if they gave up the comparison game. At least, by sticking to the comparison game, they get the joy of riding up and down on the emotional waves the game produces.

But there's more. People deeply ensconced in the comparison game have the opportunity to build an identity around their sense of being better or worse than others. When they feel superior, they feel like the expert or the superstar and set about convincing others to see them as such.

Far more often, however, the comparison game serves as the basis for a victim identity that grounds their entire approach to life. When the victim identity is firmly ensconced, it becomes difficult to break free, even if part of us would like to. Many people depend on a victim identity to tell them how to act and how to interpret life. Since for many people giving up the comparison game would mean giving up their identity, getting off the comparison-go-round is nearly impossible.

One final reason many people have trouble giving up the comparison game is that they believe it yields true information. "Why should I give up the comparison game?" they might say, "when it is objectively true that I am superior to some others and inferior to others?"

This is a good question that demands a subtle answer. Yes, it may be true that we are all inferior or superior to others along certain measures, but it is not true that any of us is inherently superior or inferior to others along every measure. Second, even if it is true that we are better or worse in comparison to others along some measures, this information tells us very little. It does not, for example, tell us anything about our character, it gives us little guidance for our decision making. It does almost nothing to develop our character.

The Profitable Comparison

The only comparison that produces growth is the comparison between our current selves and our past selves. When we look backward to see how far we have come, we can gauge the usefulness of our strategies for growth. We can assess our discipline and how effective we have been at solving problems. This kind of comparison works to let us know when and where we need to make changes, to adjust course to stay on target.

This kind of comparison also steers us away from covetousness. When we eliminate others from our comparisons, we are much less tempted to covet what they have, whether those are skills, position, praise or relationships. Rather than leading to covetousness, self-comparison can inspire us to go further, to do better, to push on toward yet unachieved goals.

At the same time, if you notice that you are comparing yourself to others, rejoice. You are doing well. Most people caught up in the comparison game are not even aware they are playing. If you are aware, you are a step ahead. The more aware you can become of this tendency, the more freedom you can achieve.

When you notice this pattern, you can reorient your thoughts in a more productive and healthful way. Whether your comparisons with others leaves you feeling superior or inferior, you goal should not be "balance." When you feel superior to someone else, the right move is not to try to "bring yourself down." When you think you are better than another, you cannot balance the scales by pointing out to yourself your own flaws. When you feel inferior to someone, pointing out their flaws to yourself will not work. This will only trigger your insecurities and flip you back into the comparison game.

No, your goal is not a more "balanced" sort of comparison, but to cease the comparison game altogether. When you find yourself caught in the comparison trap, instead of seeking "balance", seek to stop the pattern altogether. When you cease this process, your level of covetousness will fall.

Covetousness

The kind of comparison that leads to covetousness is not the same as finding inspiration in the achievements of others. Seeing an admirable quality in another, say, industriousness, and asking yourself "What if I were as productive as he?" is not a comparison that leads to covetousness because it is not rooted in the underlying sense that life is uniquely unfair to the asker. These kinds of questions don't assume the person being observed is profiting from some unfair arrangement. These questions are profitable because they assume that whatever rewards another has accrued have come to him through his own diligence.

Moreover, these sorts of questions imply that there is enough diligence, character and industriousness to go around. The fact that someone else possesses these qualities does not mean that there is less for me. When we see an admirable trait in another and want that for ourselves, we are not coveting because we do not wish to take away his good character in order that we might have good character of our own.

We can also work to become less covetous at the level of our behavior. This can be difficult because the less aware we are of our insecurities the more engrained and second nature our manipulative behavior will be. And so, we must return again to the importance of awareness.

Two techniques can help us to become more aware. The first is embracing some form of meditative practice. The subjects of meditation and prayer are vast and controversial. For our purposes, it is enough to practice simply sitting quietly, focusing one's mind on the present and noticing how well one is provided for. As we do this and as our awareness of the sufficiency of the moment increases, we find that we are more able to be satisfied and grateful for the many blessings we already possess and are therefore less motivated to compare our situation to that of others or to feel the need to "even the score."

This meditative process will also make it easier to be aware of those times when the feelings of the wounded ego come up, the feelings that drive us either to a sense of superiority or inferiority. The more consistently we notice these, the more consistently we can choose to respond to them positively.

Greater awareness and freedom allow us more flexibility in our behavior. When we act from insecurity and covetousness, most of us have a sense that we are not in line with our highest values. We know that we are not being our best selves, and that knowledge demands a response.

We can respond in one of two ways: we can repress it or we can face it. When we repress it, we become more anxious and unhappy and ultimately more covetous. Facing our motivations and learning what it feels like when we act poorly alerts us when we need to make different behavioral choices. Where we once might have tried to undermine another, to cheat him out of the full rewards of his successes, we can now do something different. We can choose to behave in ways that build up the people around us regardless of whether we see them as failures and successes. No longer is there a need to lie, gossip or behave in other ways designed to transfer from my neighbor to myself what is rightfully his.

In short, we can begin behaving in ways that show we have ceased trying to "even the score," and have moved toward a vision of abundance. When we are busy trying to "even the score," we are deeply convinced that there is not enough of good things to go around. We believe there is an upper limit to how much praise, how much comfort, how much blessing can exist in the world. We imagine that someone else having these things means there is less available for us. This leads to a plethora of poor behavior.

The person free from the scarcity mindset is free from covetousness. His behavior reflects his genuine happiness for the good that comes to others because he does not believe that good for them is ill for him. He is capable of acting in generous ways because he does not need to hoard all good things for himself because he knows that good things fall abundantly all around those who remain on the lookout for them.

And so, he is able at last to put away his covetousness. He focuses not on what others have or are enjoying, but on how he can best employ his own skills and gifts to bring light and hope into the world. As he works hard at this, his inner ground shifts. Eventually, he begins to want not merely what he sees others having. He begins to want to actualize what does not yet exist in the physical world. His most intense desire becomes to bring into being those good and positive elements that only he can bring into being and whose existence is an extension of his deepest self. He begins, in other words, to become obsessed with what he can give to his neighbor rather than what he can take from him because he sees in giving the only real and final means of "evening the score."

8

Fearfulness

The Prevalence of the Fear-Based Life

EVERYBODY GETS SCARED. MANY are scared most of the time. Mostly, this is because living is scary. It comes at us constantly with challenge after challenge. Everything from just getting up in the morning to major heath scares seems to try our courage. Some feel a perpetual knot in their stomachs trying to navigate our way through life, always wary that calamity could be lurking around the next corner.

To some extent, this makes sense. Many scary things can happen in the course of a lifetime. We could get sick. Our children could get sick. We could become disabled in an accident while running to the store because we forgot the eggs. We know this. It happens all the time. If we don't know someone who has suffered an unexpected tragedy, the news media are always happy to bring such people to our attention.

Our knowledge of how easily calamity could befall us makes living in fear a constant temptation. Living in fear becomes especially easy if we aren't good at using our reason to counter balance our fearful impulses. The more we rely on our emotions to give us information about the world, the more we will be in jeopardy of living a fearful life.

What we must remember is that our emotions are an excellent source of information about ourselves and a terrible source of information about the world. Just because something feels scary or dangerous doesn't mean it is scary or dangerous. Fearful people tend not think critically about the likelihood of negative circumstance. They instead allow their feelings to be the sole source of information about the challenges they face.

In short, their emotions rule their more objective cognitive faculties leading them to make mistakes in living. To cope with fearfulness, we must learn to integrate our affective and cognitive faculties. We can feel fear, but at the same time analyze how much that fear reflects objective reality. We can learn to calculate risk and mitigate our chances of experiencing real harm. We can only do this, however, if we are willing to break the control fear has over our lives. Getting started means reflecting on the nature of fear and determining when it moves from a good and healthy part of our lives to becoming sick and debilitating.

Healthy and Unhealthy Fear

Fear has its uses. When we approach a cliff edge, we feel fear. When we drive fast, we feel fear. When we take actions we know could result in severe negative consequences, we feel fear. In these situations, fear helps us by warning us of danger and dissuading us from doing stupid things, at least once in a while. In these situations, we should heed the voice of our fear.

Healthy fear is occasional. It comes up when we are in danger or considering some action that could cause harm. Unhealthy fear is pervasive and prevents us from doing things that are healthy, normal or fulfilling. When this happens, we have moved from experiencing normal, healthy fear to living a lifestyle of fearfulness.

People living a lifestyle dominated by fearfulness experience normal, healthy fear, but also two other more damaging kinds. In addition to healthy fear, they experience exaggerated fear over situations that do not warrant it, and they experience fear in response to their own thoughts and fantasies. This fearfulness is pathological, as all vices are, because it deters the sufferer from progressing normally in life and interferes with the process of growth.

The Dynamics of Fearfulness

Let's imagine a young man who wants to approach a woman he knows and ask for a date. A young man in a healthy emotional condition may certainly feel some tension about this, he may imagine her turning him down and feel an anticipatory twinge of rejection. Nevertheless, he knows that

Fearfulness

whatever she decides, he'll be fine. If she accepts, he'll have something to look forward to, if she declines, he'll move on.

The young man with a pathological fear habit will have a different experience. First, he will drag things out. Rather than being a simple discreet moment in time, the request for a date will likely become an event that happens again and again in this fearful man's mind. He will fret about it long beforehand. As he does so, his level of fear will increase, rising over time to meet the intensity of his imaginings.

Not all his imaginings will be negative. It would be easy to suppose that a young man with a habit of fearfulness would focus exclusively on the possibility of rejection. This is not so. Instead, he will imagine both wild success and devastating failure. The fantasies of wild success will contribute to his sense of fear as much as his visions of rejection.

The energy this young man has put into his worries has made him more fearful regardless of whether that energy takes a positive or a negative form. When he pours negative energy in, he imagines rejection. When he pours positive energy in, he imagines success. The trick to escaping his fearfulness is to stop pouring so much energy into possible future situations.

Each time the fearful man pours energy into an imaginary situation, he increases for himself the significance of the event and the importance of the outcome. His fear drives his energy which he channels mentally into rehearsing the event in the hope that these mental rehearsals will reduce his fear. In fact, these rehearsals do the opposite. By going over and over the event and imagining the woman's response, he builds himself into a frenzy.

This is not to say that when we are facing the prospect of doing something frightening or risky that we ought not prepare. The guy planning to ask for a date might wear his most flattering shirt. The guy planning to jump out of a plane wisely checks his parachute. The guy entering a martial arts competition trains. One important difference is that these preparations resolve into action. Action lowers our anxieties, endless rumination increases it.

The fearful person may ruminate due to lack of experience. Experience lowers our need to ruminate because rather than merely imagining future scenarios, we can look at scenarios from our past that are similar to the one we are anticipating. We can look at the objective facts of how we handled those situations, what worked and what did not. This allows us to link the probable outcome of the future scenario to the outcomes of the past scenarios. Doing this anchors us in the real world of cause and effect, and allows us to escape the endless rumination of our subjective fears.

Experience gives our reason something to use to reduce the intensity of our fearful emotions.

Fearful people, however, deny themselves experience. Fearful people withdraw. Fearful people make their worlds smaller and smaller until they relegate themselves to a narrow comfort zone outside of which they can barely function. This limits their experience more and more. The more they limit their experience, the fewer experiences they have to draw on when facing new and uncertain situations. The fewer experiences they have to draw on when facing new and uncertain situations, the more fear they feel. The more fear they feel, the more they withdraw. And so the vicious cycle continues.

Withdrawal and isolation then spiral out of control, constantly reinforcing themselves. At some point, something interrupts the cycle and when that happens, the fear grows intense. All sorts of things could disrupt this cycle. It could be a professional opportunity, a chance to travel, the possibility of getting to know new people. Any of these, if acted upon, could become an opportunity to break the fear/withdrawal cycle. The intensity and duration of the lifestyle of fearfulness is directly related to how frequently such opportunities to escape this cycle are taken or avoided.

These opportunities present themselves constantly. Fearful people, perhaps even more than the less fearful, are aware of these opportunities. Fearful people, however, do not tend to see them as opportunities so much as threats. Every time a chance to break the fear/withdrawal cycle emerges, the fearful person feels threatened. The threat is, in part, the possible negative consequences of acting on the opportunity. But there is another, more subtle aspect of the threat as well.

Lying within all these opportunities is, for the fearful person, a temptation. Fearful people are constantly tempted to break this cycle. At some level, they can sense that the cycle in which they are caught amounts to self-oppression. Freedom and courage want to come forward and to force change. So, the fearful person is constantly confronted by a dilemma. On one side lies the threat of new opportunities which he feels an impulse to avoid. On the other lies the temptation of new opportunities to which he desires to succumb. In this way, the fearful person spends his days in double-mindedness, highly anxious not only because of external events, but because of his own lack of inner unity, because of the war that rages in him.

The fearful person who chooses to maintain his fearfulness responds to this fissure in himself not by resolving it, but by relying again on his penchant for withdrawal. In this case, he attempts to withdraw not merely from

Fearfulness

external circumstances, but from his own internal realities. He attempts to avoid what is true about himself. Frequently, he attempts to do this through indulging in some vice that brings him a modicum of numbness and pleasure. Whether that is through drug, sex, food or other addiction, he seeks to lose himself in order not to deal with his inner cleavage, his divided inner approach to the world.

Another mode of withdrawal for many fearful people is to attempt to lose themselves in mastering an area where they feel no threat. This may mean committing to memory endless bits of useless trivia about a tv show, about celebrities, about sports. Moving toward mastery in a trivial area increases their sense of control. This process also eliminates threats for them because such areas of study rarely present opportunities and challenges to live in a new way. This process then is doubly destructive it allows the fearful to feel slightly less fearful while maintaining fear as the basis of their overall lifestyle.

This, however, is not the only vicious cycle into which fearful people easily fall. Fearful people naturally fear people. Perhaps more than any other part of life, relationships with others present both frightening challenges and opportunities. Fearful people fear relationships because at some point in their past, they were hurt by someone and their fear is a kind of hyper-vigilance designed to detect all risk of future pain.

Because of this hyper-vigilance, fearful people tend to complicate and undermine their relationships with others. Fearful people might be suspicious, distrustful, even paranoid. Quite frequently, they can be controlling as they seek to escape their fears by arrogating to themselves too much power in their relationships.

The end result is always the same. Others tire of this behavior and walk away. Sometimes they go quietly. Sometimes they do not. Either way, these ruptures create additional painful memories for the fearful person. If people walk away quietly, the fearful person may feel simply abandoned. He will likely import these fears into other relationships and project his expectations of abandonment onto new partners.

More often, relationships with fearful people do not end quietly. Given the fearful person's fear of facing life without the relationship, he may act in a manner that creates hard feelings on all sides. If the fearful person also has a penchant for being controlling, as most fearful people do, the situation might get even worse. A highly fearful person who is also highly controlling might engage in behavior that could range from awkward to unseemly to, in the worst situations, criminal, all designed to prevent the loss of the relationship.

The fearful person's negative patterns manifest themselves again and again in his relationships. Changing this pattern requires new input. He would have to gain self-awareness. She would need to improve her relationship skills. But fearful people have a hard time changing their patterns. Why? Because they are afraid. Fear is a vice, for sure, and like all really addictive vices, people cling to it in the face of mounting negative consequences.

And so, the really fearful person will attempt to withdraw even further from relationships, perhaps limiting himself to a small circle who do not challenge him much. In extreme situations, fearful people end up living hermit-like lives. With no one to counter or contradict their fearful concerns, their frightening thoughts can run wild until the person is almost entirely overcome with fearful expectations and fantasies.

How the Fear-Based Life Develops

No one wakes up one morning and says, "Well, I think I will become a terrified, paranoid hermit today!" It's not that simple. That does not mean, however, that there is no element of freely exercised choice in the process. There is.

Fearful people move toward a lifestyle dominated by fear through choice after fearful choice. At some point in life, we are confronted with an option or a course of action that frightens us and we shirk back from it. This shirking back becomes easier the second time, and even easier yet the third time. Eventually, shrinking back becomes a habit. Eventually, we find that we have even ceased to be conscious of the pattern. Our pattern of avoidance and fear has become our default response to life's challenges.

A pathological view of comfort also plays a part in the development of a fear-based lifestyle. Fearful people imagine that life should be comfortable at all times and that the absence of comfort is a sign that something is wrong. What they don't see is that true comfort only comes after a challenge is taken on and mastered. Comfort from any other source is illusory.

The desire for comfort is understandable. Life is hard. We all want some sort of respite from its troubles and travails. Yet, the fearful person ultimately deprives himself of even these. While he may stay home and may avoid other people and as many of life's challenges as possible, he does not escape worry. He certainly does not escape fear. Fear comes into his supposed place of comfort because he knows he is avoiding his duties and obligations. Sitting at home alone, he may be physically comfortable, but he'll worry about how he will pay the rent. He'll worry about whether his life has meaning. He will be troubled by endless frustrations and griefs, all because he has shirked his duties and because, deep in his heart, he knows this.

Peace in life only comes through taking right action, building a stable foundation and establishing financial, physical, relational and vocational security. But establishing such security requires serious, sometimes risky action. It requires following a course of action even if that course leads through treacherous and difficult landscapes. The fearful person is unwilling to do, and so remains trapped in his pursuit of easy, if illusory comforts while inside fears and worries mount.

And so, the fearful life is one of tension and static maintenance rather than a dynamic one oriented toward a purpose. This is one reason such a lifestyle is difficult to escape. The comfort is addicting, and the tension is so taut that there may little room to move. At least, it can feel that way.

Changing the Fear-Based Pattern

So, what's a fearful person to do? He must begin to cultivate courage. And that begins with an examination of both himself and his circumstances. Even fearful people are not uniformly fearful. We all fear some things more than others. In this fact lies hope for change.

First, look for the slack spots. Think of it this way: the fearful person lives in constant tension for the reasons just discussed. Every aspect of his life is pulled taut by his inner conflict, his fears and his drive to avoid them. The first step to changing these patterns is to look for the places that are a little less taut than others, to feel around for the slack places.

The slack places are where the tension is least great, where the fear is less intense and where the fearful person senses some modicum of freedom. It might be easy to imagine that the best way to combat a life of fearfulness is by charging directly at those things most feared. This approach has some benefits, speed being the chief one. This approach works well for situations where an isolated fear can be identified, maybe for confronting a phobia. In some of those situations, flooding the person with whatever they are frightened of can cause the fear to diminish quickly.

For a more generalized lifestyle of fear, however, this approach is not sustainable. Most people would run out of energy by the second or third attempt. Instead, to change an entire lifestyle over the long haul requires smaller attempts at making specific changes. This is why feeling around for the slack places is so important. If you are living a fear-based existence, slack places provide a clear starting point for change.

A slack place is whatever growth-producing activity you are least afraid of. Naturally, you're not afraid of sitting on the couch watching television and eating Doritos. You aren't afraid of that kind of activity because there is no challenge in it. To identify your slack spots, look for the challenge you can accept most easily.

A practical step is to write down the things that frighten you. Try to be as aware as possible of all the things that make you nervous, the things you find both challenging and tempting. When you've written down all you can think of, score them as 1's, 2's and 3's. Let threes be the least frightening and ones be the things that terrify you even to think of.

Then, move all the threes to a separate list and rank them from most frightening to least frightening. Take a long look at the least frightening thing on the list. Then, do it. Get at least something done, mark through it and pat yourself on the back. When you've done the least frightening thing on the list, do the next least frightening thing.

The goal during this process is not merely to cross things off your list, but to build confidence as you go and to interrupt the fear/withdrawal pattern. To do this, you must pursue this process mindfully. You must take stock of how this process makes you feel and process those feelings. Silence can help. By sitting in silence and attending to your sensations, being aware of what thoughts emerge for you, you can begin to reorient yourself to the present moment. Much fearfulness comes from the habit of always running forward into an imaginary and frightening future.

Learning to sit still and to focus on the present moment anchors you in the reality of the safety and security we experience most of the time. As we find ourselves more and more anchored in the present moment, we can begin attending more fully to our own feelings and responses. We can become more attuned to when we are feeling most frightened. With this awareness, you can begin to more easily work through your list of frightening life challenges.

Everything is easier at a new level of awareness. This includes overcoming fearfulness. As your awareness increases, you will notice that some of the things that frightened you once are now less frightening. You will

Fearfulness

understand more of your own responses. You will become more able to navigate through the emotions that once controlled you.

In addition to increasing your awareness, focus on increasing your skills. Some of your fearfulness stems from not believing you have the ability to handle what life presents you. You might believe this because it's true. One reason for your fear may be that in your withdrawal, you have neglected to sharpen the skills you need for succeeding in life. Without confidence in your abilities, every challenge will look more threatening than it actually is.

Ask yourself what kind of skills you want to learn. Then, think about how you might acquire or improve those skills. The good news is that most things can be learned. Even softer skills like relating well to others can be learned. You are fortunate to live in a time where information is nearly free.

One place to begin with your skills is by again assessing where you are most frightened. In what area of life do you struggle most? Is it in the professional realm or in personal relationships? Wherever you struggle most, concentrate your skills development there.

The freedom to move away from a fear-based lifestyle is within all of our power. We can choose a path in life that leads to greater fear and isolation or to risk taking, adventure and fulfillment. The doors are open. All that prevents your walking through them is the fear to which you have subjected yourself. Fear has not dominated you. There is no source outside of yourself for most of our fears. The fears you feel are largely a product of your own thinking, choosing, and habits. All those can be changed, and with that, naturally, the fear you feel can be reduced.

The world before you, in spite of how much fear you feel, can be bright, can be full of things that bring your fulfillment. They are outside the cell of your fear, waiting, calling you to come forth and lay claim to them, to make them yours. You can do it. All you need to do is to feel your fear, and resolve to take a single brave step no matter how small, and wait to see what reward, perhaps one you cannot now conceive, rises up to meet you.

9

Gossip

How Gossip Alienates

DID YOU HEAR ABOUT Tom? Linda? Sue? Patricia? How about Norbert? Did you hear about him? We can waste our lives on these questions. An obsession with what other people are doing can dominate our days to the point where we fail to make the most of our time. In effect, we substitute the lives of others for our own. We do this when we devote ourselves to talking unnecessarily about the events in others' lives. When this behavior becomes a pattern for us, we have given in to the urge to gossip. When we give in frequently to that urge, we have acquired a vice.

Gossip is a vice because repeatedly indulging in it harms our growth and that of others. It harms the gossiper by alienating her from the present, from the issues in her own life to which she ought to attend. And by lowering other people's respect for her. It harms those gossiped about by violating their privacy, lowering others' view of them and undermining their ability to operate confidently in the world. All these conditions encumber the human capacity to grow.

Defining Gossip

Before we examine the damage gossip can do, let's try to say what gossip is and is not. Gossip is addictive because, like all addictive substances and compulsive behaviors, it distracts us from our present problems and offers a temporary relief that inevitably makes those problems worse. As such, we can learn to distinguish what gossip is in part by noting the kind of talk that has addictive qualities.

Here are some things that are not gossip: discussing a relationship problem you have with a third party in a sincere effort to gain insight and make positive changes, informing someone of necessary information about a third party for work purposes, divulging non-private information about a third person while relating a personal anecdote to a friend or colleague.

Here is what gossip is. Gossip is the relating or discussing of the personal details of the lives of third parties who are not present for the purpose of gratifying the need to feel important, included, powerful or superior. So, for example, telling a work colleague that Joan said she was working on a sales report is not gossip. Telling a work colleague that Joan spent a fortune on her new shoes and that she thinks she looks so hot in them is.

The Need Behind the Chatter

The impulse to gossip comes from a lack in the gossiper. When we inhabit our own lives less than fully when we are alienated from our present, we begin to look around at others' lives. The emptier our own lives, the more intense our addiction to gossip is likely to be. This inner lack can present itself in various ways.

Some people feel this emptiness as loneliness. Without connection to significant relationships, they gossip to feel involved in the lives of others. By telling tales or discussing details of others' lives, they nurture the illusion that they know others well. They also gossip to represent themselves as more connected to the subject of the gossip than they are, to demonstrate their insider status.

The emptiness can also be felt as anger. Some talk about others behind their backs to vent anger in a way that seems safe. They may talk about people who are not present because they are angry and yet frightened to express themselves directly to the person at whom they are angry.

This anger may be legitimate, but often it is not. If we are angry about an offense that has damaged us directly, that has cost us something significant, reputation or hurt feelings, then we may have real grounds for being angry. If the issue is merely that we find someone annoying for petty reasons, we are in another arena altogether.

I once worked at a place where everyone got along pretty well. Everyone on the staff seemed to enjoy one another's company, with one exception. Some people really disliked the janitor. One coworker, in particular, resented the janitor for, in her opinion, failing to clean adequately. At some point prior to my starting to work there, the janitor began reporting to the manager trivial mistakes the staff made. This behavior culminated in the janitor reported to our manager that the flip-top on the dishwashing liquid in the staff kitchen had been left flipped up overnight instead of being flipped down.

It is hard to imagine a more trivial "offense". And yet, this became the subject of much angry gossip. I know because I heard it. This anecdote reveals an important truth: angry gossip moves in more than one direction. The janitor gossiped to our manager when she reported the offending dishwashing liquid lid. The manager gossiped to the staff about the janitor's report. Then the staff gossiped about it with each other. One of the problems with gossip is that it spreads to become an inclusive net of complaints, often only half-true, if that.

This process hurts people. The damage to their reputations is not complete in a single back and forth interaction. Instead, in these situations, a single action detonates a gossip bomb whose reach can go far beyond the initial conversation. The aftermath of these gossip bombs can also easily destroy people's reputations, careers, and in extreme instances, even their lives.

Gossip can also be a way to manage stress and build group cohesion. People like to feel included and reassure themselves of their place in the social world by sharing news and opinions about others. Talking about what is happening within our group causes us to feel reassured about where we belong. By participating in these discussions, we demonstrate our loyalty. When we talk about problems in the group, we have an opportunity to contribute to their solutions.

Sometimes the problems in our groups involve people or personality conflicts. When we talk about these, we necessarily talk about people, sometimes people who are not present. All these behaviors have benign and malignant forms. It is important that people talk about problems, even interpersonal ones. Reinforcing one's role in a group is also important.

Things stray into vicious gossip when one of two things happens. One is when talk ceases to be about the group and becomes the expression of one person's anger against another. In the case I described above, we can see what I mean.

In that case, one person in particular carried a grudge against this janitor. Her focus on this woman's shortcomings was intense. So intense, in fact, that we have good grounds to believe it was about something other than a tattle-telling janitor. In this particular case, the underlying issue seemed to be a general fury at the unfairness of the world. Her relentless gossip about the janitor seemed like an attempt to make things right, as if by lowering this janitor in others' estimation, she could somehow reverse the hurtful pattern of her experience in the world.

Second, these things become vicious when the talk becomes incessant and a substitute for actual problem solving. The goal of group discussion of problems should be to find solutions. When criticism or vindictiveness or complaining become ends in themselves, our talk has become toxic. In these situations, the talk itself becomes the problem. Only a concerted effort to stop it will now solve the problem.

The Costs of Gossip

Toxic talk like this hurts not just its target, but everyone involved. In these situations, gossip generates energy that spirals downward into greater and greater negativity. This negativity becomes palpable and grows until the entire organization suffers. Gossip hurts not just the person gossiped about, nor even just the gossiper. Left unchecked, it can even bring down entire organizations and derail them from accomplishing their missions.

Negativity is in an inherent quality of gossip. No one believes that sitting around saying nice things about someone counts as gossip. To be gossip, there must be a sense that we are sharing something private, something that if made public would damage the target or something that would be hurtful in some other way. At the core of gossip is betrayal and a desire to enhance our own emotional lives through enjoying the salacious details of others' lives or of seeming to be "in the know."

This is obviously the case with what we call "celebrity gossip." Discussion of celebrities and their private lives has been common since the advent of mass media and entertainment. From movie star magazines in the early 20th century to TMZ.com today, the persistent popularity of celebrity gossip tells us much about what kind of people we are.

The widespread appeal of celebrity gossip makes it is even easier to see our propensity to gossip. Most of the millions who enjoy celebrity gossip don't know a single celebrity. This highlights something important about the nature of gossip. We like it because it is remote from our own lives, from what we are living in the present.

Gossip does not require us to risk anything personal. When we engage in gossip, we enter into an emotional fortress from which we can take shots at others while being perfectly protected ourselves. In the case of celebrity gossip, we can tell ourselves that being gossiped about by us is part of the price celebrities pay for being rich and famous. Our obscurity, we think, entitles us to a few free jabs.

And yet, our proclivity for celebrity gossip tells us we are not wholly satisfied with our obscure little lives. Our obsession with lives so remote from our own indicates a dissatisfaction with what we are, what we have. It indicates a longing to be something like what we imagine celebrities to be. By focusing on celebrity gossip, we are able to have a feeling that we move among this vaunted elite. When we talk about celebrities as if they're our friends, we deceive ourselves into feeling as if that may be true. We feel elevated as if we have moved from our own obscurity to the reflected glory of their fame.

At the same time, we get the feeling of being superior to the people we are talking about. They may be rich, famous, and beautiful, but we have the power to run them down as we sit in the hair salon or at our desk at work. This gives us a sense that not only do we hold a position in this elite group, but that we are among the elite of the elite whose power exceeds even that of those we read about in the glossy magazines.

All this also conveniently allows consumers to avoid dealing with the difficulties and problems in their own lives. When we devote ourselves to the discussion of others' behavior, we feel it gives us an out from accepting responsibility for our own. Some will happily let their lives fall apart so long as they can focus on someone else's foibles.

Celebrity gossip also allows us the feeling of ripping the mask off someone, especially someone we perceive to be rich, powerful and privileged. Unmasking our target seems to confirm for us what we've always suspected: that people whose status is greater than ours are, behind their shining edifice, no better than we.

This doesn't just apply to celebrity gossip, of course. We take great relish in exposing those we perceive to be above us in our own life. Think about how delicious it is to gossip about your boss, about the girl more popular than you. Not only do we have a sense of reducing what we believe to be their undeserved status, we elevate ourselves, or think we do, in the minds of our listeners. We imagine gossip as a kind of status equalizer that lifts up the lowly and brings low the proud.

Underneath all this is a lack in our sense of ourselves. We look outward and turn other people into symbols of our inner deficiency. Regardless of whether this deficiency comes out as angry or lighthearted gossip, an extensive pattern of gossiping about others tells us something unflattering not about them, but about ourselves.

When we cultivate a habit of talking about others in this way, we communicate that we cannot be satisfied with what life has afforded us, that we are not able to be satisfied, above all, with our present selves. The right response to dissatisfaction with ourselves is either self-acceptance or change. Both of these paths are demanding. To accept what we dislike about ourselves requires an enlargement of perspective, a willingness to accept not just ourselves, but the flawed nature of all reality. It requires a willingness to live in freedom from the tyranny of our imagined perfection and unreasonable expectations and to come to love what is real.

Changing requires just as much work as accepting. Changing requires accepting that social reality is governed by principles, and that one of them is that talking poorly about others always yield negative consequences. It means finding a way to bring our behavior and thinking in line with those principles. It means facing the reality of our previously faulty thinking and behavior.

Gossiping is much easier than either accepting or changing. That's why the number of people who gossip is greater than the number of people who either accept themselves or change their bad habits. If change or acceptance were easy, everyone would do it. Instead of pursuing either of these paths, most people distract themselves by focusing on others failings, It is as if they believe others' problems excuse their own. We would do better to stop talking and to start working. Wasted time, hard feelings and stagnation, these are the true costs of gossip.

Gossip and Anxiety

Gossip serves us in other ways as well. Think about the times when you are in a circle of people who are gossiping. One reason we gossip is simply that it gives us something to talk about. It is hard to overestimate the amount of anxiety some people feel when making simple conversation. Talking about other people is like having a crutch to lean on. Some people, when the conversation lulls, experience a kind of inward panic, borne of not knowing what to say or how to keep a conversation going. Having a healthy reservoir of gossip helps such people feel better when they cannot think of what to say next.

Eventually, these people become addicted to gossip as a means of relieving their anxiety. The problem is that, as with all addictions, negative consequences mount. In this scenario, the first negative consequence is that when we gossip, we undermine others' trust in us. When we talk about others who are not present, those to whom we are talking eventually begin to wonder if, when they are not present, we might talk negatively about them. Their guards go up. They begin to view us with suspicion. That suspicion eventually corrodes our relationship with them destroying the very thing we were trying to build.

Moreover, the content of what we say in those conversations can always leak. Casual conversations are not airtight containers. The people to whom we gossip are not sworn to secrecy. They may repeat what they've heard. They may even repeat it to the target of our gossip. Knowing this may be a cause for even more anxiety. Being worried about the possibility of some unkind word we've spoken getting back to the subject of our gossip can add to the anxiety we feel about relationships. Increased anxiety is thus a symptom of the damage we do to ourselves through talking negatively about others.

But the damage we wreak in these situations doesn't just hurt us. By gossiping about others, we inflict hurt as well. What we say in private does not necessarily remain private. When our private words become public, the consequences for everyone involved can be steep. Those who find they've been gossiped about suffer. They might feel betrayed, might be hurt to learn their actions and intentions have been misrepresented, perhaps maliciously and intentionally. This is especially true when the gossip is found to have been lies intentionally spread. The damage this kind of gossip can do is untold.

Gossip-free Living

Fortunately, it is not necessary to engage in gossip. People can live well without it. Since gossip is neither necessary for survival nor for the good life, we ought to make every effort to avoid it. How can we do that? Avoiding gossiping must be done with some finesse or else we may become the target of gossip ourselves. If we are too confrontational about our desire to avoid gossiping we could hurt others and, as we have seen, most people are inclined to deal with their wounds through gossiping.

The first step to avoiding gossip is simply to become a person who does not gossip about others. To do this requires changes both internally and externally. Internally, we must become separate enough from our circumstances to be free not to care too much about the political workings of our environments. The first solution to the gossip problem is distance.

One good way to get this distance is to develop a personal sense of mission and purpose. People who aren't clear on their reasons for being in a relationship or in a work environment easily fall into gossip. Becoming clear on our reasons for the things we do and on how the things we are doing fit with our long-term plans does a lot to free us from the grip of our immediate circumstances.

Imagine a young woman at work where there is a lot of gossip. Let's say her long-term goal is to own her own bakery, but for now she works in a supermarket bakery section learning the basics of making cakes and bread. Spending time every day running down the people in the deli behind their backs is a trap and a distraction for her. If she falls into that trap her energy becomes invested in something other than in extracting the value from her experience that might help her realize her long-term dream.

When she gets caught up in gossip, she neglects learning the details of mass-production baking. She focuses more on what other people are doing than on what opportunities she is being afforded at the moment. If she gives in to an unhealthy focus on the details of others behaviors, she will be distracted from being the best possible employee, which will mean depriving herself of future opportunities.

Getting very clear about where we are going will help avoid these pitfalls. Think of having a clear mission as a destination that when you have it, allows you to draw a line from where you are to where you are going. Sticking to that route allows you to avoid the snares, like gossip, that slow many travelers down.

Having a clear long-term goal also puts immediate circumstances into a perspective that can make gossip less appealing. Take our hypothetical baker. If she is focused on making her dreams a reality, then she can see that where she is at the moment is a passing and transitory phase of her overall journey. When she is focused on getting the things she desires and on using her current experience to bolster her chances, interest in gossiping about the cashier's love life naturally wanes.

Doing this sort of internal work reduces our need for the stimulation gossip provides. But that may not be enough. Even if we are inwardly free from a need to follow the details of others' lives for entertainment or to wreak subtle havoc in our relationships, there may still be social occasions where a more relational approach is needed.

Let's imagine you are at work and a co-worker begins gossiping. What do you do?

Well, one thing not to do is to say, "Hey, look, that's gossip and I don't listen to gossip!" Responding this way almost guarantees disaster because it conveys that you have an opinion of yourself as being above what this person considers to be normal. That's not a good impression to leave with others, especially if this co-worker is also your boss.

There is no reason to respond in such a direct and confrontational way when there are many other possible responses. We should instead regard gossipers with compassion. We must see them as seeking to fulfill a real need, even if the way they are seeking to meet it is damaging.

When we see this, our purpose in the conversation shifts. We see that we are no longer there to protect ourselves from being tainted by hearing gossip, but to elevate the situation. One way to do that is simply to reflect back to the person your observations about them. So, if a co-worker is angrily gossiping about another, you might say something like, "Wow, that really upsets you."

These situations require sensitivity. If you feel that your relationship with the gossiper warrants it, you might try gently inviting him to examine himself by saying something like, "Do you know what it is about this that upsets you so much?" In this way, you invite your interlocutor to look at his motivation for gossiping, and potentially decrease his drive to do gossip in the future. These are just a few strategies for dealing well with this situation. Others would work too.

Whichever strategy we choose, we will be affirming our decision to forego gossip. By renouncing our penchant for gossip, we ground ourselves in the present. Rather than focusing on the details of far-flung liaisons and vague complaints, we can focus on accepting and cherishing what is. We can especially focus on our own character and where our virtues could stand to be burnished. In all this, both the internal and external work, we are moving toward becoming people who bring a sense of justice and safety to the world. Both these are sorely needed, and just as their cause can be served by what we say, it can also be served by what we do not.

10

Resentment

Unforgiveness and Resentment

As I mentioned in a previous chapter, unforgiveness has serious consequences. If we refuse to forgive long enough, a wall forms in our hearts, a hard, immovable structure we erect out of our sense of having been wronged. We hold onto grievances and nurture new ones. We build the wall brick by brick. Eventually, it casts a shadow over everything we encounter. It darkens our vision and makes it hard for us to see with any real accuracy.

When we reach this point, unforgiveness has become resentment. Unforgiveness and resentment are clearly related, but the subtleties of their origins and effects differ significantly enough that each deserves its own treatment. Resentment is the result of cultivating an attitude of unforgiveness over the long haul. When we allow resentment to take over, it changes the sort of person we are.

Resentment and the Lack of an Ideal Life

Unforgiveness, I established earlier, is a maladaptive response to the hurts we experience in life. Resentment does not spring solely from hurt, but springs more fundamentally from disappointment. Life did not go as we expected it to go. Our plans did not work out. We did not get the job we wanted. We could not afford to attend the school our hearts were set on. The woman we wanted rejected us. Such is life.

When we cannot accept these losses and instead tell ourselves that we are owed a life that is easier or in some way better, we become filled with resentment. Resentment is a broader concept than unforgiveness and goes to the heart of our relationship with reality itself. Resentment is ultimately about our disconnection from reality and our alienated relationship with our own inner sense of the ideal.

A person filled with resentment may have suffered betrayal or have other legitimate grievances, but it is not necessary that this be so. A resentment-filled person can simply be a person whose life experiences have been entirely normal, but who once became entranced with a particular ideal of life and, when that ideal failed to materialize, became resentful.

Sometimes early in life we pick up, either through being told directly or through indirect means, a sense of what our lives will be like. We develop images of what will be coming our way. These images are rarely negative. No one wants to spend his time imagining a dark future for himself. We naturally filter those things out and focus our minds on the beautiful and positive futures we find beguiling. Our expectations take shape and begin to harden.

All of this is good in so far as it motivates us to work hard to achieve the outcomes we imagine. If we work to make manifest what was once only an idea, then we are on the right track. The problem comes when we become overly attached to a single one of these images of the good life.

The Problems of Being too Attached to Our Vision of the Good Life

Becoming overly attached to a single image of the good life creates many problems. When we come to believe that only one particular mode of living can satisfy us, we set ourselves up for trouble. We believe that we are more likely to bring about the imagined set of circumstances by focusing on them intensely to the exclusion of all other possibilities. This is not necessarily the case.

Let's begin by looking at the nature of life. First, we must reckon with the reality that life is hard. In spite of the universal and overwhelming amount of evidence for this thesis, most people remain in denial of it. Naturally, this denial makes life all the more difficult. Accepting that life is difficult can actually make the difficult realities we experience slightly less difficult because it removes from us our sense that hard things are abnormal or unusual.

And yet, many never accept this. Instead, they form an attitude toward life which provides fertile soil for resentment. Rather than accept that life is difficult, some people cling, no matter what, to the idea that the difficulties they experience are an aberration from real life, something unusual and out of place in the world. Their refusal to accept the difficulties of life does nothing, of course, to make life less difficult.

When we go through life under the impression that each negative experience is somehow an aberration from what life is "supposed" to be, we cannot help but find an unending stream of evidence for our hypothesis. Every negative event we encounter provides one more point of data to bolster our conclusion. Each painful moment makes it clear to us that we have been dealt with unfairly by life and whatever power governs it.

This pattern of thinking produces an unhealthy focus on others. When we refuse to believe that life is, by its nature, difficult, and yet we continue to experience difficulty, it is a simple thing to assume life is only difficult for us. The falseness of this assumption does little to dissuade resentful people from believing it. When we take our painful experiences to be deviations from the way life is "supposed" to be, and we compare our lives to what we imagine others' lives to be, we lose.

The inevitable result is to conclude that for others life is more the way it is "supposed" to be. When life works better for others, at least in our estimation, we come to resent not only life itself for its unfair treatment of us but others for somehow benefitting in the cosmic lottery in a way we did not. We compare our experience with what we see of others' lives, and feel that we have gotten the short end of the stick. Our anger grows.

As our anger grows, it shows in our behavior. We begin to show our resentment in the form of destructive behaviors whether they be overt of covert. We may get into fistfights or simply devolve into a person who routinely makes subtle cutting remarks to put others down and "even the score." Evening the score is of utmost importance to resentful people.

Because they tend to imagine that life has dealt more fairly with others than it has with them, it's easy for resentful people to take upon themselves the burden of addressing this wrong. Resentful people often have little trouble justifying their bad behavior. The idea that because life has been unfair to them, they are allowed to be unfair to others works as an excuse for all kinds of bad behavior.

The Score Cannot Be Evened

The resentful, of course, cannot even the score because the score cannot be evened.

Attempting to even the score is futile for two reasons. First, because in spite of wildly differing privileges and situations people all suffer internally. Resentful people tend to underestimate the inner suffering of others. They judge others based on shallow criteria and make shallow assessments. They believe that others are better off internally than they are. Rarely do they see the deeper suffering which is present in all lives. Because we all suffer internally, even perfect fairness in our material conditions would not eliminate our difficulties. Even in that scenario, our levels of inner anguish would differ.

Second, fortune simply favors some more than others. It has always been thus. Thus, it will always be. This truth is an expression of the larger truth with which this chapter opened: that life is difficult. That it is not always as difficult for some as it is for others does not negate the fact that it is difficult to some degree for all. No amount of labor designed to even this score will work because that project is at odds with the fundamental nature of the world we are thrown into at birth.

Trying to even out the suffering in the world is an excellent way to waste a life. Such a quest is bound to end in frustration because its object can never be attained. The further down this road the resentful travel, the more resentful they become because again and again they find their efforts stymied. Whoever pits himself in battle with reality will lose. The resentful rarely learn this and so pile up for themselves a string of regrettable losses.

Those losses often come in the arena of personal relationships. Potential spouses spurned, professional relationships ruined, families strained all because the resentful person continues to run in the well-worn circles of his anger. Each of these losses however is also an opportunity. Each one represents the chance to turn back from nurturing resentment. Each one represents the chance to adjust the lens of perception. Each loss is a chance to move out of the resentful frame of mind into one more balanced, compassionate and fair.

Resentment

The Opportunities in Our Losses

People who take advantage of the opportunities that loss affords them have a reasonable chance of improving their situations. People who do not will continue down the road of resentment until their losses become so extreme, they find themselves isolated from others and without resources.

To some ears, the idea that loss affords opportunities may sound strange, but it's true. In fact, learning to see these opportunities is instrumental in overcoming resentment. The resentful mind, because of its disappointment with existence, trains itself to look for evidence that confirms its bias toward negativity. This pattern of bias confirmation narrows the perspective of the resentful mind until it can scarcely any longer perceive contradictory evidence. When loss comes, even a loss brought on by his own attitudes and behaviors, the resentful person can only see that loss as further evidence that life, the universe and everything is arrayed against him.

Learning to contradict these thoughts, to examine his underlying assumptions is an important step toward virtue for the resentful person. Entertaining the idea that his narrative of disappointment and mistreatment might not be the whole story is like cracking open a door in a pitch dark room. Even if only a little light gets in, more is visible than it was only an instant before. The ability to see more of reality arouses a curiosity in the mind. This curiosity, in turn, leads to a desire to explore and to see more of reality as it is. The willingness to see reality as it is is a necessary first step away from resentfulness.

This applies even more fully to situations where we have experienced loss. Loss hurts. It's natural that we would want to blame another for causing it. Often, others have caused our losses. But when we view our losses only from the darkened perspective of our resentment, we will be unable to see that the changes our losses entail afford us chances to capitalize on new abilities and skills, to form new relationships, to gain new insights, to establish new habits and to reach a new level of growth.

Blame is Resentment Made Manifest

Instead of stretching themselves, resentful people cultivate blame. Blame is the unfair attribution of responsibility to another. In order to further understand the role of blame in resentment, we must distinguish between it and responsibility. Someone once said responsibility is taken while blame is given. This maxim captures an important element that separates the two. Responsible people accept their agency. They see their lives as fundamentally products of their own making. They see their situations and circumstances as emerging from their perspectives, attitudes, thoughts and actions.

People who blame do the opposite. They see their circumstances, to the degree that those circumstances are negative, as being largely the fault of other people's choices and actions. They see themselves as merely acted upon by other players in life. They live in reaction to what they perceive to be the accumulated slights they've received at the hands of others. They believe their major problem is that others will not take responsibility for their misdeeds.

Their blaming serves two purposes. First, it functions as yet another attempt to even the score by telling others what responsibility they should take. When they confront and blame others, however, others balk. The other person may deny the charges. He may offer an alternative interpretation of the facts. He may eventually just disconnect from the blamer entirely, leading to one more incident the blamer can use to confirm his conviction that life is slanted against him.

Resentful people take others' resistance to being blamed as proof that they are right in their blameful assessment. If others were willing to take responsibility, the resentful person reasons, they would accept without question all the blame assigned them. The resentful are eager to get others to accept blame because they assume the pain they feel is always someone else's fault. The solution then, they imagine, is to control and change the other. The problem, the resentful person assumes, is that others never own up to the pain and hurt they have caused, and so they must be made to do so.

That others do not willingly accept blame is evidence, in the mind of the resentful person, that they are immature and cannot be trusted. The fact that the resentful person did trust once and was hurt then becomes even more evidence that life is a series of disappointing circumstances which then intensifies the resentful person's basic resentment of reality.

None of this can be worked out through conversation, of course. Blame precludes productive conversations. In order for conversations to enhance connections between people, both must take responsibility for their thoughts, feelings and behaviors. When this happens, people can work together to come to mutual understandings and negotiate for mutually acceptable arrangements. Blame is a repudiation of this process. Rather than aiming at building mutually satisfying agreements, blame is about gaining power over another.

People being blamed know this. No matter how the resentful person seeks to hide his power agenda, it becomes clear. When it is clear that the resentful person is seeking power rather than connection, the resistance of his target intensifies until the relationship ends.

The Flawed Logic of Resentment

One reason resentful people often end up bitter, alone and miserable is that they never learned to think in nuanced, complex ways. They have trouble seeing life from another's perspective and find it difficult to believe that others' perspectives, agendas and needs are as valid as their own.

Flawed thinking is also one of the roots of their fundamental disappointment with existence. Rather than approach life with a mindset that emphasizes nuance, complexity and a multi-factorial approach, their basic orientation is simplistic. Rather than seek objectivity and a multi-perspectival understanding of reality, they emphasize emotion. When they feel bad, reality is bad.

The idea that feelings give a total assessment of reality, though wrong, is understandable, especially in the cases of people who have experienced early trauma. When our early lives are characterized either by intense, inescapable pain or just a grinding negative atmosphere characterized by criticism, harshness, and lack of warmth, we come to rely on our feelings to keep us safe. In these cases, our feelings work as a kind of distant early system alerting us to threats which might injure us further. Eventually, we leave the threatening environment. Unfortunately, although we leave the situation, we rarely leave our habits.

Resentful people thus carry with them through life the inclination to trust their feelings over the insights of others and even over their own capacity to reason. Because they feel betrayed by existence, existence must have betrayed them. Without opening themselves up to outside information, without finding some reality they will trust more than their own feelings, they remain stuck.

Resentful people are attached to their feelings. They identify with them. They believe they are their feelings. This fact is fundamental to many attachments resentful people make, and to the way they manage those attachments.

Their pattern of attachment management sets them up for resentment just as much as does the fundamental disappointment with existence.

Resentment and Over-Attachment to Expectations

Before we go further, let's talk about what an attachment is. An attachment is simply an emotional clinging to any object, person or situation. We all have them, and we must all manage them. Most people are able to manage the breaking of an attachment relatively well. They may feel bad for a while, may sit at home and cry, may eat ice cream out of the container, but eventually, they let it go.

Resentful people are less good at managing their attachments. When a broken attachment is forced on the resentful person, they fight. If they can't fight, they sulk. One way or another, they seek to keep the attachment intact. It is as if they believe that by keeping the attachment alive, they can forestall the pain of losing it.

We all get attached to our expectations. We get an idea in our head of how life should be, of how life will be. In the vast majority of instances, life doesn't turn out in a way that matches our expectations. How badly this upsets us is a measure of the strength of our attachment.

Resentful people have never been able to let go of their attachments to their early expectations of life. When life did not meet those expectations, rather than adjusting and moving forward, the resentful try to avoid the pain of giving up these early expectations. One function of their resentment is to maintain some connection to those early hopes. It is as if they believe that by refusing to let go of the resentment, their hopes may yet materialize.

And yet, letting go of these early dreams is critical for overcoming resentment and opening up to life. We all form dreams when we are young of how our futures will be. Sometimes these function well for us, serving us as imagined destinations, a compelling if hazy vision of where we would like to go. These dreams help us to guide our decisions and thus guide the results our choices yield.

This process can go wrong, however, when we become overly attached to a particular vision of how life "should" be. We must realize that these visions were formed when we were very young and not yet clear on how the world works, when our values were not yet fully formed, when our ability to assess what truly matters, and when our capacity to strategize about achieving those things are not fully developed.

Resentment

Moreover, these dreams are often not really goals, but emotional projections, fantasies about a future life where we will be free from the pain and trials of our current one. If we have experienced trauma in early life, our plans for our future, rather than being realistic and functional, can easily become not so much plans but images we carry with us of a life that addresses through its ease and comforts the losses we have sustained in the past. The hurts of our past can warp our expectations of the future.

Letting go of resentment means giving up this habit of dealing with the hurts of our past by raising our expectations of the future. Instead, we must accept what is, what has happened to us. We must accept that very often life does not live up to our expectations. We must take the disappointment we feel and dispel it by opening to the good-enough life actually available to us.

At the bottom of every resentful heart is the question of whether a life which fails to conform to the expectations we place on it can be meaningful, whether when we are denied the fulfillment of those early dreams we can still find a mode of living which brings fulfillment. The good news is that we can.

Even in the worst of conditions life remains meaningful. Psychiatrist Viktor Frankl became convinced of this while in a Nazi concentration camp. One day while working as forced labor laying railroad tracks, Frankl wondered whether there could be any ultimate meaning to human life. Suddenly, he heard a voice he could not identify answer him with a resounding "Yes!"[1].

We have the opportunity to offer this same enthusiastic response. The first step to doing so is to look at the events of our past and to distinguish between those we can do something about and those we cannot. Obviously, no one can undo the events of the past, but that doesn't mean we must do nothing. We can decide how we will live with them. We can explore the meaning we assign to them. We can decide how we will respond.

This is all true for the negative experiences we have been through. Even though these experiences are in the past, we can do much in the present to mitigate their effects. Our ability to ameliorate these effects, however, depends largely on our basic attitude toward life. The less willing we are to accept the realities of life, the less capable we will be of managing the effects of our negative experiences.

---

1. Frankl, *Man's Search for Meaning*, 41

This is so because when we refuse to accept the basic nature of life, its difficulty, its unwillingness to comply with our wishes, we become resentful , and though it may make us feel strong, resentment disempowers us. The more we resent the basic, unchanging nature of life, the less we are willing to take responsibility for our own choices within the parameters the nature of life lays down.

So, the first step to becoming less resentful is to accept the conditions in which we find ourselves. "Accepting" is an abstract notion and something difficult to know how to practice concretely. So, a better approach may be to focus on something easy to practice which in turns shifts us toward a more accepting stance.

The chief of these approaches is to practice gratitude. At first glance, "gratitude" might seem as abstract a thing to practice as "accepting," but it really is not. We can practice gratitude by making it a point to thank others more frequently. We can make lists. We can silently count our blessings. Do this enough and the truth about how well provided for we are will become clear. This is not some sort of self-trickery, but a balancing of our vision. Because, though the resentful may see the disappointing aspects of life clearly, they ultimately see only half the picture.

11

Understanding Virtue

The Other Side of the Coin

Now that we have looked a while at vice, it is time to turn the coin over and look at the other side. None of us comes into the world already virtuous. What virtues we possess, we acquire as we grow. Examining a few in detail will enhance that growth and move us more quickly along the path leading to them. Having examined the dynamics of common vices, we now need to consider some virtues worth cultivating. Let's get started.

To begin, let's ponder the differences between a vice and a virtue. There are several. The first is that a vice requires no training to develop. All of us can easily develop vices simply by giving in to our nature. Take sloth as an example.

Vice Comes Naturally

Our bodies require little coaxing to sit around and be comfortable. Nobody disciplines himself to get up early in order to settle down on the couch and eat Cheetos. No, we do these things because they feel good immediately. Whenever we fall into a pattern of doing exclusively what yields immediate good feelings, we lose part of the order of our lives. The habit of repeatedly doing only what feels good immediately is vice.

We need challenges to grow, and the pattern of always seeking immediate good feelings is a pattern of avoiding a challenge and thus, of avoiding growth. Notice that the development of a vice has two components.

First, vices grow from behaviors that offer immediate gratification in the form of good feelings. But good feelings alone do not define a vice. To truly acquire a vice, we must repeatedly turn to these behaviors to help us get through the day.

Remember that both virtue and vice are habits. When we repeatedly turn to instantly gratifying behaviors, we develop the habit of depending on them and thus move from a simple indulgence to a full-blown vice. Of course, the development of a full-blown vice has antecedents, factors that have come into play that make us vulnerable to developing these bad habits in the first place. We looked at some of them in the first half of this book. In short, we have problems and we naturally turn to behaviors that help us escape rather than solve them.

Because turning to immediately gratifying behaviors comes naturally, so do vices. What does it mean to say that vices "come naturally?" It means that if we follow our own impulses without some intervening force or motive that drives us to embrace difficulty, we will end up in vice.

Virtue Must Be Practiced

Virtue, on the other hand, requires effort. Virtue does not come naturally. Virtue is cultivated, meaning that we must make intentional, meaningful efforts to make it grow. No one taught you how to be selfish. No one took you aside as a child and gave you some pointers on how to become a person who prioritizes immediate pleasure above all things. You were born knowing these things.

However, if you were fortunate enough to have any kind of moral education at all, you must have experienced the opposite. At some point, someone corrected your behavior. Someone instructed you about the right way to behave. When you behaved in a positive way, you may have received positive feedback. When you behaved in a negative way, you likely received negative, perhaps even harsh, feedback.

The point is that you were taught how to behave, how to conduct yourself according to certain standards, standards which you, left to your own devices, would not have adopted. In short, virtue is not natural in the sense that it comes to us without effort. Rather, it is a product of the social and spiritual dimension of the human person.

Imagine that all your vices are weeds that spring up spontaneously from the soil of your soul. These you must remove. You must sift through the jumble of vegetation and remove what is ugly, dangerous or otherwise unwanted. You did not plant these weeds, they appeared there unbidden. Virtues are like vegetable plants. They must be planted, cultivated, nurtured to full maturity before bearing their fruits.

Two Reasons We Pursue Virtue

Since it is the case that virtues are not, in this limited sense, natural, why do we pursue them? For a couple of reasons. First, as I said previously, if we are fortunate, we will have received some moral training. This training is not merely externally imposed. Rather, the purpose of the training is to pull out of us something already there. I will talk about this more in a moment, but first I want to address the reason of why we continue to behave virtuously, to the extent we do, even after our moral educations are long complete.

The purpose of our moral educations is not merely to teach us right from wrong. Their purpose is deeper. The purpose of a good moral education is to teach us how to behave and to help us to make good behavior automatic. When we choose virtue again and again, we become habituated to it. We take on habits that, through practice, become second nature. These habits can be so deeply rooted in us that they shape the way we see the world. Thus do virtues which began as imposed expectations on our behavior become an intrinsic part of the way we perceive reality. When this happens, acting contrary to them would be acting contrary to the very core of what we think reality is.

This is the force of habit, a power that helps carry our quest for the virtuous life forward. We have formed a habit when we routinely behave according to a certain pattern without thought. Habit frees us from the need to consider every decision. When we are in the grip of a habit, we do not deliberate, we do not launch into an inward debate with ourselves about each and every option before us. Instead, we choose at a subconscious level.

This process can produce good or bad results depending on what kind of behavior we have been habituated to. This is why early training in virtue is so important. When our moral education begins early, we have the opportunity to begin habituating ourselves to choose the good from early on. By no means is it impossible to do this later in life, but we may find it is more difficult to do without the advantage of early models and teachers pointing us in the right direction from the beginning.

The question of training in habits leaves some questions unanswered. Consider these: Why do people allow themselves to be habituated toward the good? Why do people continue to make virtuous choices even when they are no longer under the power or control of those early teachers to whom they were once forced by size, strength or circumstances to submit? Why do children often come to see for themselves what is virtuous? How does an external pattern of training and correction eventually become an internal moral vision? What makes the standards once externally imposed take root in the soul? Habits can be passed down, but how is it that a moral vision so deeply rooted that it becomes the lens through which reality is perceived get passed along the generations?

The answer to all these questions is also the second reason we pursue virtue. Our embrace comes about because, though conditioning is important, it is not enough. We are not the kinds of beings who operate on mere conditioning. Our conditioning is only part of what determines our choices and behaviors. Even from our earliest days, our training is not merely the imposition on us of our parents' will or a code of expectations laid down on us by the larger culture.

This is so because deep inside us, we all carry a sense of moral ideals. We all have an inward sense that some choices are good and some bad. We certainly know when we are being treated in ways we ought not be treated. We also have an internal sense not only of what is good, but of what every virtue and good character trait would look like taken to its farthest point. In short, we have a sense of the perfection of every virtue.

Because these ideals dwell within us from birth, they form the second part of the equation regarding how we are able to become virtuous people. When our parents or other teachers train us in virtue, they may appear to be merely imposing a standard on us, but they are not.

The standard already exists in our minds and souls. This, however, does not mean that we can or would choose to conform our behavior to it if we could. Rather, we must be trained to choose those behaviors which align with the ideals we already know intuitively. Our moral educations are not just about imposing a standard externally, but also about amplifying the strength of our inchoate moral intuitions.

Because we naturally intuit these inner ideals, we can be trained to bring our behavior in line with them without resentment. Because we know the ideal or principle at which our choices ought to aim, we can know that when we are asked to choose the good, we are not a victim to some more powerful person or force, though we may be pushed by external forces to conform our behavior to an ideal, the ideal itself is not just a construction or an arbitrary expression of another's will to which we must bow.

Training in virtue therefore is training in how to live in accordance with ideals that were already in our minds long before any training had begun. As we act in ways that approximate these ideals, we understand them more and more. Eventually, our understanding of these ideals becomes the foundation on which our worldview rests. Thus does early, external moral training become a deeply rooted internal moral vision.

Vice, Virtue and Our Place in the World

This worldview influences our inner experience as well as our observable choices. The connection between virtuous behavior and inner peace is clear. When we behave in ways that are consonant with the Ideals we reduce degree of inner conflict. Our level of self-respect goes up. When we feel that, in spite of our imperfections, we are acknowledging our inner ideal we trust ourselves more. We can then take a relaxed attitude toward life, toward existence itself.

The opposite is also true. When we behave in ways out of line with the Ideals our level of internal conflict rises. We begin to feel guilty. We begin to deny what we know inwardly to be true. Our relationships deteriorate. We lose respect for ourselves and others. We cease to trust the ideals to lead us to be something better than we are.

When we experience this inner chaos, we often choose to try to escape it through behaviors that move us further from the Ideals. Eventually, we may begin to resent the ideals, or to pretend they are not there. We risk sinking into an abyss of cynicism and harshness from which we may never rise.

In this way both the path toward peace and the path toward chaos reinforce themselves. Through our choices, we can set up for ourselves either virtuous or vicious cycles. Both become difficult to break. But, in most instances, only people caught in vicious circles desire to escape them. This is because vicious circles hurt. For the reasons described above, vice can lead to chronic internal and external pain. Admittedly, there may be cases in which acting in accordance with virtue might cost one something, a relationship, a job or some other valued thing or circumstance, that pain is fleeting, and is usually accompanied by a sense of pride and peace that comes from having remained faithful to one's values in spite of pressure to do otherwise. And thus is virtuous behavior reinforced.

You can think of these reinforcement cycles as upward and downward spirals. The virtuous circles tend, over time, to lift people to new levels of understanding, insight, maturity and productivity. The vicious cycles, on the other hand, tend, over time, to drag people down into greater levels of resentment, fear and dissolution.

This fact should move us to take our actions and decisions seriously. While no one can fret about every action or choice he makes, most of us err on the side of not taking our behavior seriously enough. Given what we know about the spiraling nature of vice and virtue, it should be easy to see why this is a mistake. Each choice we make, each behavior we engage in, can be one more step in a process that ultimately determines our level of satisfaction with ourselves, our peace of mind, and our overall happiness.

Most of us end up floating haplessly somewhere between the poles of vice and virtue, in a place we did not plan on being. This is because rather than think seriously about our characters, rather than make conscious decisions about the kinds of people we desire to be and how to become them, we allow circumstances to make decisions for us. We float along on the surface of life, never taking control of the ship of our own moral destinies.

"Well," you might ask, "if that means we end up between the extremes becoming neither saints nor demons, what's wrong with simply going with the flow?" The answer is that virtue is profoundly tied to meaning. As we develop the habit of choosing the good, as we pursue virtue, our lives and choices become more meaningful. We develop both a deeper understanding of the import of our decisions and of the way their effects ripple outward in positive ways into the lives of others. As we experience this, our sense of meaning intensifies.

On the other hand, when we repeatedly choose vice, our vision of what makes life meaningful grows obscure. Our self-centeredness, bitterness, anger, fear and so on cloud our ability to see both the gifts we have been given and those we have to give until eventually the world seems dark, random and ruthless. Through this vicious cycle we become demoralized, lost, and harsh. In short, the vicious cycle make us vicious.

In the end, our vision of the world and how it works is, an expression of our choices. If we routinely make choices that elevate ourselves and others, we are more likely to see the world, in spite of its pains and challenges, as meaningful and holding some measure of glory. If we routinely make choices that lower our spirits and harm others, we are more likely to see the world as dark, dangerous and corrupt. In short, we see the world as we are.

Circles, Virtuous and Vicious

The goal then is to get ourselves positioned in as many virtuous circles and as few vicious ones as possible. Another fundamental truth about the difference between virtue and vice makes this difficult. The first steps toward virtue rarely feel good, but the first steps toward vice almost always do.

So, initiating a virtuous circle is difficult because the first steps don't feel good. They may even hurt. For this reason, we must figure out some means of keeping ourselves going during those first few instances in which we are setting up this new pattern. One way of doing this is simply not to allow ourselves to exaggerate the difficulty we encounter.

Let's say you wanted to extend your self-discipline by breaking your addiction to sugary, caffeinated beverages. This might be tough at first. Depending on how long you have been drinking these, it might be very tough. If youre body is conditioned to expect a certain amount of caffeine every day at a particular time, you may find yourself with a headache when that time comes and you don't engage in your usual indulgence. Even if you don't get a headache, you might have a craving for a soda you will have to deny. You might have the craving almost constantly at first. Your self-denial will have to be equally constant.

To get past this, simply step back and realize that these hurdles are not as high as you might believe. In these situations, we tend to have emotional reactions to what we anticipate the change will cost us. If we step back from our reactions, we can see that in most instances, these costs can more or less be shirked off. If we consider these objectively, we will see that they are negligible and we can move on toward our goal without much difficulty.

We can also tell ourselves that impulses to revert to the behavior we are trying to stop will come, and we can plan for them before they arrive. The best way to deal with these kinds of situations is simply not to think much about them. In this example, when the thought of a cold soda presents itself, the best thing to do is to acknowledge the thought and move on to a different thought.

Temptations of all sorts worsen and intensify the more we struggle with them. The more we wrestle with them, the stronger they become. Think of it this way: vice wants your attention. It will happily take it in any form. If it cannot get your attention by having you engage in whatever behavior you are trying to eliminate, it will gladly take it in the form of having you think about how much you would like to engage in that behavior.

To get out of this predicament, just give vice no attention. Decide ahead of time you will not deliberate with yourself over whether or not to engage in this behavior. Make a firm and final decision. If you are willing to enter into a debate with yourself about whether or not you will engage in the behavior you have decided to eliminate, you are merely playing at having decided. A true decision to end a behavior brooks no internal debate. If you do find yourself in an internal debate, end it quickly. This is how you show that your decision was firm and final: by not entertaining even the possibility of justifying going back to the old way.

Finally, you must remember that virtuous circles are reinforced by the positive consequences of our actions and that the only thing that brings about positive consequences is taking action. In order to feel the positive consequences that will reinforce your virtuous circle, take action as quickly as possible. Immediate positive action will bring the positive results that will keep you going. Set yourself up with some easy wins when you are trying to build a good habit. Begin your quest with some actions that yield immediate positive, tangible rewards, and work from there.

The flip side of this process is escaping a vicious circle. The first step in this process is acceptance, particularly accepting that as disconcerting as it may be, you have gotten yourself into a trap. Denying this helps nobody. You must recognize the progressive nature of the cycle, and acknowledge that stopping a vice now is the only surefire method to prevent it from metastasizing.

This truth offends our sense of ourselves as the kind of people who don't get into trouble. But the only way to break out of a negative and self-reinforcing cycle is to lay aside the ego's concerns and to look at reality squarely. Only once reality has been faced and we've taken stock of the consequences of our negative behavior can we find the necessary motivation to break the cycle.

While it is true that facing the negative consequences of our previous choices might be unpleasant, it is critical not to linger in shame or guilt or despair. It is particularly important not to succumb to self-recrimination. None of these things is adequate motivation to change. In fact, all of them tend to undermine the success of any attempt to break these cycles by reducing our conviction that we are capable of change.

Understanding Virtue

Far better is it to focus on the future and on what you are bringing into being than on what you are ending. Only think about what you are ending when it is necessary, but as much as possible set your mind on what is higher and let yourself be drawn toward it.

Now, the hard part. There is no way to change except by actually changing. The pursuit of virtue happens one choice at a time, and the escaping of vice means making different choices in each moment where life presents us a choice, which is to say in every moment. While the fact that life is presenting you a choice between vice and virtue at every moment may seem overwhelming, on another level it is a source of great hope. We know that whenever we make the wrong choice, another opportunity arrives in the next moment.

Training oneself to be aware of these moments is critical for escaping a vicious circle and pursuing virtue. When we see the choices before us, we can choose more consciously what kinds of action most reflect our values. Becoming aware of this forces our minds and souls to enlarge.

Vice flourishes within a narrow mind, confined by its habits and unreflective. As we think more about our behavior especially while we are in the middle of it, we create greater awareness for ourselves and open up our consciousness. Opening up allows us more freedom to choose. This too is a self-reinforcing cycle.

When starting the process, start small. Pick some small pattern of behavior where vices routinely creep into your life, and determine to root that pattern out. Spend your day trying to be aware of when you are about to engage in whatever vice you want to eliminate. If you must indulge, do so with forethought and deliberation as this is still better than living life on autopilot with limited consciousness.

Finally, focus on actively cultivating virtue where you can. Familiarize yourself with the virtues you want to pursue. Pursue them regardless of whether or not you succeed or fail at your attempts to squash your vices. Meditate on what is good. There are many resources to help you including the following pages of this book. Come along now as we explore some of those virtues which make human life truly human.

12

Discipline

Discipline: The Foundation of Virtue

I'M BEGINNING THIS CHAPTER after having taken a break from writing. For about 15 minutes, I snacked and surfed the internet. Eventually, the time came to get back to the business of the day. I chose to continue with the work before me rather than to escape it through another snack and more YouTube videos. I made a conscious decision to keep going with a project that is demanding and which offers little immediate reward. I made that decision as an act of faith. I believe this book will one day be finished (if it is in your hands, my faith has been validated) and that all sorts of goods will come from having finished it.

This process is the essence of discipline. Discipline, especially self-discipline, is a cornerstone virtue, meaning that without self-discipline, all the other virtues become impossible to attain. We have looked at what an undisciplined life looks like in some of the previous chapters, the ones on sloth and self-indulgence come to mind. Now, it is time to consider the reverse image, a picture of the well-ordered life.

Discipline as Adherence

First, though, we must know what discipline is. Discipline, contrary to one popular conception, is not punishment. Punishment is when an exterior force intentionally brings pain or difficulty into our lives as a means of dissuading us from repeating a certain course of action. Discipline does not

Discipline

necessarily mean pain or difficulty, though, of course, it may. Discipline really means adherence to a set of teachings. That is why one who follows a particular teacher is sometimes called a "disciple." Self-discipline is the internalization of a set of teachings to the point where we no longer need the teacher to be physically present. We do not require punishment because we are now capable of living out those teachings on our own, applying them even in private when no one is there to see. We are self-disciplined when we do not need anyone to tell us to act out these principles and teachings, but rather do so from a genuine desire on our own part to see the doctrines to which we have committed manifest in reality: and when we look forward to the good consequences we anticipate our disciplined choices will bring. As we do this, our connection to what makes life meaningful increases. But there is a cost.

The Price of Self-Discipline

As everyone who has ever tried to achieve anything knows, discipline is not easy. What's easy is choosing to avoid our goals. Sitting at home and neglecting our projects is easy. Choosing again and again to return to work, to act in line with a well-defined goal is not easy. Allowing our actions to ramble all over the map is easy. The hard thing is to stay on the path we decided to pursue back at the beginning.

Discipline may be hard for us for a few reasons. First, we may not have fully internalized whatever ideas are guiding our actions. This is very common. We may think we have internalized some set of teachings, but if our behavior does not reflect these principles, we have not.

To change this, we must realize that we are always acting on some set of internalized beliefs. We are always accepting some sort of discipline. We are always bringing our behavior into line with a vision of the world that governs our moment-to-moment choices. Even if we are the most slovenly and slothful of persons, we are this kind of person because we have embraced a set of ideas that tell us this is a sort of person worth being.

To adopt another kind of discipline, one which might lead to a new set of choices and more positive consequences, we must accept and internalize a new set of doctrines. Fortunately, human beings are capable of conscious decision making. Unlike other animals, we are capable of stepping back from our behavior and asking what set of beliefs lie behind it. It is through exercising this capacity that we find our way to exercising all our others.

Discipline Is Not Willpower

It should be noted here that discipline, just as it does not equate to punishment, equally does not equate to willpower. It is not the case that some people have been born with an extra helping of whatever mysterious trait allows them to force themselves to do what they know they ought. Instead, people we see as having extraordinary willpower are people in whom the conditions for self-discipline have been met. When these conditions have been met, self-discipline appears. To those who possess it, this self-discipline seems not like an extraordinary exertion of the will, but like ordinary life.

Discipline's Necessary Conditions

What then are the conditions which allow self-discipline to occur?

We have discussed the first condition a little already: the internalization of a code of conduct. Also necessary are proper motivation which allows us to feel that we have the power to act on this code even in the face of our fears, challenges and obstacles, and faith that through acting on our internalized codes we will be part of bringing into being a set of circumstances which will yield important and positive results for ourselves and others and enhance our connection to meaning.

If you want to develop self-discipline, proper motivation is crucial. Too many people fall into the trap of thinking themselves incapable of self-discipline, unlike others whom they imagine to be far more capable of disciplining themselves. This, however may not be the case. Many people have simply never connected a motivating vision to consistent positive actions.

Fear: The Motivator of the Majority

Instead, many people are motivated by one thing: fear. People we might consider hard-charging "type-A" individuals and people who avoid all challenges can share this motivation. Fear can easily wear self-discipline as a disguise. The person whom we look to as a paragon of discipline and self-control may, in fact, be a person who, at his core, is simply consumed by fear. His discipline and focus may in fact be driven, not by adherence to a code of conduct, a sense of meaning, or a set of teachings. All his outward discipline might be driven by his fear of lack, of embarrassment or catastrophe.

Discipline

The person who, owing to a lack of self-discipline, has not experienced the kinds of success he would like may be just as fearful as the one whom society regards as more "successful." Inwardly, the more successful, more driven man may be just as unhappy as a slothful man. Fearful motivations have a way of equalizing people.

Both the undisciplined and the disciplined man must connect with their own meaningful visions of the good life. This vision exists in each of us. This vision, when we behold it clearly, can serve us as a guide. It points us the right direction. It makes clear what we must choose if we intend to arrive at some approximation of it.

Though this vision exists in every soul, not every mind is conscious of it. Many simply dismiss their images of a more meaningful life as a pointless fantasy, some unobtainable dream. Of course, when we dismiss our inner magnetic draw to a certain sort of life, we also dismiss the very things which motivate us to take consistent action toward bringing into physical reality what now exists only in the mind. In other words, we dismiss the very things that motivate us to be self-disciplined.

If self-discipline is the willingness to take consistent action to achieve a goal in spite of obstacles and without an external force compelling us to do so, then the motivation for that consistent action must be internal. The man with little self-discipline is likely a man who has dismissed the things that would truly motivate him and seeks instead to go through life powered by fear, necessity and social approval.

When those shallower motivations fail to motivate us adequately, as they inevitably must, the pattern of choosing changes. The man with shallow motivations returns repeatedly to behaviors that do not advance him toward his goals. Instead, he allows the world to distract him, lead him to waste time, to wander from the path to his ultimate destination.

Immediate Comfort is the Ultimate Distraction

While undisciplined behavior does not lead us toward our goal, it does offer immediate comfort. Moving towards one's vision of the ideal life, even of the ideal self, is difficult. Obstacles present themselves at every turn. Walking that road is hard work. It is much easier to simply give up and revert to some other plan which requires less difficulty and promises less satisfaction.

It's easiest to see these truths illustrated in the arena of physical health. What is true for the body is true for the soul. Though our visions of our ideal life vary from individual to individual, no one's vision of an ideal life contains poor health, sickness or suffering. No one thinks, "In my ideal life, I would bedridden in constant, racking pain". So, while the details of individual visions might vary, some elements, including physical health, are universal.

So, since we all share physical health as part of our ideal vision of life, we all hope to maintain our current level of health or to progress toward a better one. While we are not, of course, all experts in diet and exercise, we all have a basic level of knowledge that tells us that some things are healthier than others. We all know an apple is better for us than a candy bar, that water benefits us more than beer.

Since 1) Good health is universally desired and 2) all of us have some basic knowledge of what is better and worse for us with regard to that end, the question arises: why do so few actually improve their health?

The answer is that most have not sufficiently connected to the desire for good health strongly enough to carry them through the temptations they face daily. Here's how it works. Most people desire better health, but only in an abstract way. They imagine themselves looking better, feeling better, enjoying themselves more. Then comes the time for action.

Most fall out of the race at this point, never even getting off the starter's block. Their desire for better health remains purely mental. When making some actual change is required, say, something as simple as resolving to drink more water, they balk. Their abstract understanding of health is too weak to overcome the inertia of the comfort of lying on the couch. Because drinking more water requires intention, memory and expending the energy to walk to the sink, they give up and go on through yet more of life as dehydrated as ever.

The next group of people stick with their resolutions a little longer. They actually walk to the sink and down an extra glass of water. They forego the cake at work. They talk a walk two days in a row. Then things get tough, something happens that demands a response from them, their stress levels rise. Unable to tolerate stress, they walk into the break room and down a couple of slices of the now day-old cake.

One poor choice makes the next poor choice easier. Soon, our subject is sliding right back into the same vicious cycle she was trying to escape. This scenario illustrates that the problem is not simply lack of will power. Our subject here sincerely wants to improve her health. Her will is engaged. She wants this.

And yet. Her wanting it is not enough to see her through the difficult and stressful moment where she makes a choice contrary to her goals. In order to get through this moment, her commitment to health must be less abstract to her. The only way to make it less abstract is for her to connect further with the vision of the person she wants to be, her vision of a more meaningful life.

How to Connect with a Motivating Vision

She can do this in a couple of ways. One is to make her mental vision of her ideal life and self more tangible. She might sit down and visualize these things in as great a detail as possible. She might imagine what being her ideal self, in her ideal place would look like, sound like, feel like, etc. She might also write down what she is after. The more she writes down her vision and returns to what she has written, the more concrete that vision will become in her mind. She could tell others about her vision, collect images that help clarify what she wants. Anything she can do to lend some sensory depth to what heretofore had been a mere mental construct is going to increase her connection and thus her discipline.

The second way she can increase her connection to her vision of her ideal life and self is to act right now. Our subject is likely to feel some disappointment in herself, some guilt or shame as she exits the break room where two slices of cake have now vanished. At that moment, she has another decision to make, she is at that moment confronted by another test. She must decide whether her next action will move her back in the direction of her goals, a path which is more challenging to walk, or whether she will allow herself to slide backward toward the old habits in which she has been ensnared.

The best way for her to get back on the track to her goals is to act immediately. Even at work, she can ask herself, "If the person I want to be had just eaten two pieces of cake because a deadline is coming up, what would she do next?" Then, she can do that thing. She can take some immediate action that manifests the qualities she wishes to cultivate. Even if her options in that moment are limited, she can at least choose to drink a bottle of water or take a walk around the office. She can show herself that the eating of the cake was an aberration rather than the norm. She can show herself that she is really the kind of person who drinks water and moves a lot. She can make a mental note to remember this moment the next time she feels stressed and to make a different choice when that moment comes.

Immediate positive action, no matter how small, makes our journey toward our ideal selves more real, more concrete. Then, rather than merely depending on "will-power" to carry us through, we can rely on the tangible real world results our actions create. This is why immediate action is so important. Immediate action creates immediate results. Immediate positive actions create immediate positive results, and immediate positive results speak to us and tell us who we are.

As her connection to the as yet unrealized vision of who she wants to be begins to become real, she will find herself encouraged, and this newfound spiritual lift will carry her onward and power her through the next test. Eventually, she will come to a point where what now seems like an intense test becomes trivial. She will power through obstacles that once delayed her without noticing. This is the power of the virtuous cycle.

The second condition necessary for self-discipline to take place is faith. I am not saying only religious people can be self-disciplined. I am saying that to bring into existence realities that are now only mental, one must believe that there is a connection between actions and results. This may sound obvious, but with a little reflection, we can see that this connection is often broken.

Imagine a young boy, a teenager who gets his first small job. Each week, his boss pays him a few dollars which the boy folds and slides into his pocket. Every week on his way home, a bully accosts him and steals the money. Eventually, this boy begins to think that working is not a valuable use of his time because he never gets to enjoy the fruits of his labor. He may slack off at work or quit outright. Doing so, of course, would likely get him labeled as someone who "lacks self-discipline", when in reality, he is a person for whom the connection between his positive choices and the feedback they provide been broken. His lack of hard work is a sign of his flagging faith.

We can see this same dynamic at play in other, more subtle ways as well. It happens often in schools, for example. When a student who sincerely tries to do well and makes a good effort is criticized publicly, made to endure some punishments arbitrarily doled out by a presumptuous teacher or otherwise harassed, bullied or undermined, this connection is broken. This is just one of thousands of possible examples.

When I say the connection is broken, I do not mean that the person involved ceases to have an intellectual understanding of the fact that actions bring about consequences. I mean that the connection is broken at

Discipline

an emotional level. In these situations, we cease to feel that the connection between actions and consequences is tight enough to really matter. We suspect that even if we try to bring about a desired outcome or earn a particular reward, others will intervene to prevent this process from reaching its natural conclusion.

The result of this is a process of 'checking out.' Someone who feels this connection has been broken eventually simply gives up trying to bring about his desired outcomes. He drifts through life because he has become convinced that any discipline he undertakes will ultimately result in a lost investment.

The first step then toward a more disciplined lifestyle is a recovery of faith. This requires a process of reconstituting the connection between choices and outcomes. He must test reality and become convinced that even if the process is sometimes interfered with, the cause-effect relationship maintains its integrity more often than not.

To do this, he must imagine some small reward he'd like to earn or some small positive result he'd like to bring. The importance of thinking small cannot be overstated. People trying to develop discipline. tend to become overwhelmed easily and lose the will to persevere. Rather than determining to clean the house and keep it spotless, scaling back to just making the bed each day would be a better plan. If making the bed each day is too big a challenge, scaling back to merely throwing the blankets across it in a less sloppy fashion is an option. The project itself matters less than that it be small enough to keep him going.

Each day he must complete this small task until he begins to see the rewards it brings. Straightening blankets on the bed yields immediate results because it moves the bedroom from looking terrible to looking less terrible with only a few seconds of effort. Other rewards will come, too. Eventually, straightening the bed each morning will become automatic and its maker's mindset will shift to thinking, "I am the kind of person who makes his bed."

By repeating this process, his faith in the relationship between his action and their effects will gradually be restored. He will cease to see himself as powerless and begin to see himself as a force shaping reality. This will be the sign that his faith in the idea that the connection between cause and effect is real has been restored.

Even someone less skeptical about the relationship between cause and effect, may still desire to live a life of increased discipline. That is entirely possible. If that's you, here are a few ideas to consider.

If you have done what is necessary to connect to a motivating vision, then determine what you desire to be disciplined about. Too often people approach discipline as a blanket issue. Trying to move from an undisciplined, chaotic life to one of rigid order too quickly is a recipe for failure. Instead, pick some task or area of life and make it your focus. You might begin by drinking more water every day or taking a walk at lunchtime. Pick one thing and focus on developing your discipline around it.

Discipline necessarily involves doing a thing repeatedly. To earn the benefits of consistency, you must be consistent. You must be consistent until your new habit forms fully enough that you cease to think about it. There are a few ways to do this. One way is to do whatever action you want to turn into a consistent habit as early in the day as possible. Check it off your list before you are swamped with distractions and obligations. When you know that you have taken care of whatever it is you promised to do for yourself, you can roll through the rest of the day knowing it is behind you and that you are one step closer to developing discipline in that area.

When you feel tempted to disregard your new discipline, use your temptation as a sign that you should avoid whatever is tempting you. This requires a new level of self-awareness. Rather than being inside your temptations rather than identifying with those thoughts, learn to recognize when you are thinking them. As soon as you recognize them, do the opposite of what those thoughts are telling you. Learn to see your temptations and inner debates as flares sent up by an enemy who does not want you to live a disciplined life. Undermine his efforts whenever possible.

However you get there, you must accept that discipline is the path to peace. If your life is frenetic, overwhelming or feels pointless, look at your discipline. Are you disconnected from your real desires? Have you ceased to believe in the connection between cause and effect? If so, and if you want something better, it's time to rebuild those connections. All you have to do is choose to do so over and over again. Eventually, you will notice that you have moved further than you expected in the direction you desired to go. You will notice you are more of the person you wanted to be. You will see, in time, that you are not just making your decisions, but that they are also making you.

13

Sober-Mindedness

Getting Sober

HARDLY ANYONE USES THE word "sober" in its older sense anymore. When we hear this word used now, it mostly means "not intoxicated." This usage, naturally, is quite prevalent in circles of people overcoming drug and alcohol addictions. In these circles, it is not uncommon to refer to abstinence from intoxicants as "sobriety". Someone who is breaking an addiction to alcohol or other drugs is said to be "getting sober." All this is fine, of course, but regardless of whether we have problems with substances or not, sobriety in its older sense is a virtue we all should cultivate.

A quick check of dictionary.com offers a good view of these older, more expansive meanings. There, we see that while "sober" is indeed defined as "not intoxicated," it is also defined as "habitually temperate" and "marked by seriousness."[1] All people should strive for habitual temperance and seriousness since these traits are hallmarks of maturity.

Because sobriety in this sense is an indication of maturity, we should not be surprised to notice its marked absence in our society. Contemporary American society is a very unserious place. We are unserious because we have lost any scale of meaning. When we cannot adequately assess the meaning of things, we cannot rank those things on a relative scale. We cannot know what is very meaningful and what is trivial. We cannot know to what we ought to attend and what we ought to ignore. We cannot be sober-minded. We have lost our connection to any ideal of maturity.

---

1. https://www.dictionary.com/browse/sober

We no longer know what seriousness is. Many people when hearing this word assume it means humorlessness. Even worse, some assume it means arrogating to ourselves the right to inspect our neighbors' behavior for minor infractions and to bring them back in line. This is not correct. Being serious does not mean being life's hall monitor. In fact, as we shall see, people who aspire to be life's hall monitor are often deeply unserious.

What it means to be sober-minded is the opposite of what it means to be frivolous. Sober-minded people are not those who never celebrate, who never experience joy, who grit their teeth and clinch their fists to get through life. Rather, they are people who take life with all its challenges and opportunities, as we would expect, seriously.

A few chapters back I talked about the scene I observed once at a large gathering of homeschooling parents. The men leading the event all wore oversized silly hats to conduct the meeting. This was not an example of sober-mindedness. Their behavior was not consonant with the occasion. Rather than conducting a meeting characterized by an adult mood and setting a tone that reflected the serious work of educating one's children, these men approached the situation in a way that communicated that they saw the proceedings as less serious than they obviously were. In their role as leaders, their behavior encouraged others to take the situation less seriously, too.

This attitude makes itself felt in other areas of our lives as well. Having spent more than a decade in teaching college students, I can say first hand that a lack of sober-mindedness is rampant in higher education. In a typical situation on campus, the students do not want to learn. They lack any serious purpose for being in college other than those few who might be focused on getting a job afterward. Many faculty are equally unserious, consumed with politics or focused on trivial details of administration or the implementation of new programs.

What is Sober-Mindedness

If sober-minded seriousness is not joyless harping on the failings of others, what then does it look like? It looks like the mature ability to assess the meaning of events and to respond with an appropriate level of meaningful action. When a situation is serious, sober-minded people take it seriously. They keep level heads and refuse to react with intense, unwarranted emotions. They make situations and life events neither more burdensome nor more trivial than they warrant. Sober-minded people assess reality and are able to choose the best response from the myriad available to them.

This process entails at least two distinct components, assessing and responding. When people are not capable of sober-mindedness, it is usually because something has gone wrong in one of these areas.

The Ingredients of Sober-Mindedness: Objectivity and Charity

Assessing reality rightly means two things. First, it means pursuing objectivity. While none of us is ever entirely free from having what we want to be true shape what we believe to be true, we can with effort make great strides to seeing reality as it is. We can value what is true more than what, if true, would most conveniently advance our personal agendas.

This is harder than it may seem. Being sober-minded requires overcoming as much as possible the pull our desires exercise on our understanding. Doing so requires a willingness to sacrifice our desires to truth, and that willingness requires a commitment to maturity. Because sober-mindedness is connected to maturity, let's imagine an example involving that universal symbol of immaturity: the teenager.

Let us say a teenager, we'll call her Lindsay, wants to go out with some friends. Let us also say her mother tells her she has to be home by her 11 pm curfew. Lindsay can accept this maturely as a sign of her mother's care and concern for her, or she can respond with less maturity. If she chooses the latter path, she might tell herself that her mother is unnecessarily controlling. She might tell herself that her mother only wants her to be in by 11 as a way of keeping her from fully experiencing her teenage years. She may tell herself her mother is only setting a curfew because she is controlled by her fears and that she, Lindsey, has a right to her own life, one not dominated by her mother's baseless anxieties.

In this situation, Lindsey is likely to misinterpret her mother's intentions. Chances are high that she will misinterpret them intentionally. Lindsey may conclude that her mother is unfair, that her mother is motivated only by concern for herself, or that she does not have a realistic grasp of how the world works. Of course, reaching these conclusions makes Sarah feel justified in ignoring her mother's instruction to be home by 11.

If we look more closely at Sarah's pattern of thought, we will learn something more about sober-mindedness and its relationship to maturity.

One sign of immaturity in Sarah's thinking is that she arrives at her conclusions first. She wanted to justify ignoring her curfew, and thus she constructed a line of reasoning to achieve that end. She made the point of her thinking something other than truth and wisdom and thus rendered her thinking subject to her immaturity. Her thinking keeps her locked in a loop of immaturity.

Lindsey also made a mistake by framing the as issue one of her mother's character rather than of evidence. It is theoretically possible that Sarah's mother could be a controlling, self-centered woman who only wants to soothe her own anxieties by laying down a curfew for her daughter. To know whether that is true we would need to see the evidence. This means looking at Sarah's mother's past behavior. Has she normally shown real concern for Sarah's well-being? The fact that she allows Sarah to go out with her friends at all seems to serve as evidence that she is not so overcome with anxiety that she will not allow her daughter a normal life.

Whatever the evidence reveals, Sarah's mistake is not considering it at all. Most people, like Sarah, ignore the evidence in these sorts of cases because the evidence counters the conclusion they have already decided must be reached, counters the narrative that most serves their agenda. This is not maturity, nor is it sober-minded.

Her lack of sober-mindedness does not bode well for her relationship with her mother. The pursuit of objectivity allows us to join with others in finding reasonable and workable solutions to problems. Two people whose thinking is directed at justifying their own agenda, at finding some means to get their way, can never come together around a shared solution. Two people who are willing to be as objective as possible have a much higher chance of reaching a mutually satisfying solution to their differences.

Had Sarah thought objectively about her mother's imposition of a curfew, she might have understood that being home by 11 would allow her to get enough sleep to function well the next day. She might have realized that the later she was out the higher her risk of an accident might grow. She might have seen any number of good reasons why being home by 11 was in her best interest.

Beyond both the need to think objectively and the need to consult the evidence, sober-minded maturity requires a recognition of the other person's concerns, perspectives and desires as legitimate. Sober-mindedness requires charity. It means understanding that nothing becomes good simply because we desire it. Sober-minded, mature people recognize that situations are often comprised of people with differing interests and agendas and accepts these as legitimate.

What does recognizing legitimacy look like? It looks like assuming that the other people involved are being up front, that their motives are good and that their perspectives deserve to be heard. Sober-minded, mature people do not cast unwarranted aspersions, even mentally, upon those with whom they negotiate. By granting legitimacy to others, we find we are able to transform interactions which otherwise would be power struggles over competing agendas into cooperative efforts to reach mutually satisfying compromises.

Our Cultural Context

In addition to these personal roadblocks to sober-mindedness, many of us simply cannot really conceive what living a sober life might mean because of our cultural context. We live in a culture that distrusts sobriety. This is why the men I described at the homeschool meeting wore those ugly hats. Though clearly they had failed to assess the situation clearly and objectively, they were also laboring under many cultural assumptions that led them to treat the situation without reverence. For example, many people share the common cultural assumption that the worst thing others can believe about them is that they take themselves seriously.

Because a pronounced anti-seriousness subtext permeates out culture, sober-mindedness is often perceived as an indicator of self-conceit, of thinking more of oneself than one ought. The train of thought seems to go like this:

1. Everybody knows that the only things worth taking seriously are the things that empower you to consume. Thus, it is acceptable to take our health, our jobs and our finances seriously.

2. Taking seriously anything not directly related to consumer power indicates that you think you know more, that your values are important, truer or somehow better than the consumerist values others have embraced. Sober-mindedness indicates that you think you are better than your neighbor.

3. Therefore, people who take things other than consumer power seriously are really deluded about how important they are. They think they're special.

4. People who believe they are special are necessarily wrong, and need to be brought down and to have their egos deflated.

Most people in our culture accept this chain of thought even if they are unaware of doing so. The result is widespread fear of appearing serious in order to avoid being thought self-aggrandizing. In order to avoid communicating seriousness, many make efforts to signal the opposite. They look for ways to convey that they too believe the words they are saying, the actions in which they are engaged, or the duties which they are discharging are not very serious. Their belief that proper comportment ought to derive from the opinions of others rather than from the meaning of our task makes evident their lack of sober-mindedness. The result is a culture without gravity. In a culture with no gravity things fly away from one another leaving behind only chaos.

This chaos is where most people now dwell. It is the milieu in which their minds and souls and characters come together. They take its bedlam as normal and the pattern of unseriousness grows as people replicate what they see around them.

As a result, we end up with a population that could not be sober-minded if it wanted to be. The ability to take life and the situations we meet in it with seriousness has not been inculcated. Their seriousness skills are in need of serious attention. The personal costs of this are huge.

The Costs of Our Culture

We pay for our inability to be sober-minded in a couple of ways. We pay by blundering into situations and patterns that damage us and others. Consider the arena of dating and marriage. People who view one another only as vehicles to fun and pleasure and affirmation can't help but harm one another in the long run. It is only by seeing one another as unique souls worthy of serious attention, respect and honor that we can begin to create relationships where we might feel at home.

This dynamic also shows up in our use of humor. Most people enjoy others who see the funny aspect of life, who laugh and are able to make others laugh. No conflict exists between being sober-minded and serious and being humorous. When employed with insight and sensitivity, a gift for wit and cleverness can express our appreciation for life and even make important points that guide people and improve their lives.

Sober-Mindedness

But when used without the capacity to take others seriously, humor can easily become destructive. If we repeatedly make fun of someone or joke about topics they have asked us not to joke about, we are not taking them seriously. We may be unaware that this is the case, but the damage still gets inflicted. Through our lack of sober-mindedness we have failed to take other persons seriously and thus blundered into a scenario where we have hurt the relationship, sometimes irreparably.

Even this is not the most costly way that our lack of sober mindedness hurts us. We pay in a second, more significant way. Just as we can easily fall into a pattern of damaging others by not taking them seriously enough, we can hurt ourselves by losing opportunities because we simply do not take ourselves, our callings or our lives seriously enough.

At some point in life, people begin to sense this. Their failure to take seriously their lives and missions leave them feeling stuck. Their feeling stuck then gives rise to all sorts of other negative, difficult emotions. A paradox hidden in the quality of sober-mindedness is that only by taking our lives seriously can we begin to go through life lightly. Those who do not take their lives seriously are often anything but light-hearted. They are often racked with worry or eaten up by bitter anger.

Eventually, these negative emotions cloud the ability to see fresh opportunities to move forward. See, opportunities present themselves most clearly when we take our callings most seriously. When we are most determined to get somewhere, the path becomes most clear. Lack of seriousness about our lives and their potential for good has the opposite effect.

People who do not take seriously their lives and opportunities wander aimlessly. They waste time. They squander the chance to achieve and so build little because of their unseriousness. They do not see themselves as a force, as a person with mass and weight that can be thrown behind a good cause.

Not uncommonly, people who fail to take themselves seriously often do so because they were never taken seriously by others. Often, especially when we are young, we internalize what we think others' opinions of us are. If we get the message that we lack enough value to cause others, especially those most important to us to take us seriously, we likely won't take of ourselves seriously either. Instead, we will feel disempowered, incapable of doing good. We will not see life as serious. We will shrink before any serious calling.

This insight therefore brings us back to the first point: that we do damage by not taking others seriously. Our lack of sober-mindedness and seriousness is a disconnect from meaning, the meaning inherent in our lives and actions. When we operate from this meaninglessness, we establish a vicious cycle where, because we do not take ourselves seriously, we encourage others not to take themselves seriously either, and so they, in turn, do the same. All the while the opportunity costs of missed chances grow higher.

All this brings us at last within proximity to an answer to the deepest question on this topic: Why be sober-minded? Why be a serious person at all? The answer is that in spite of all its difficulty and pain, life is a gift. Each one of us has had life bestowed on us from outside ourselves, been given without regard to any prior merit the opportunity to experience the wonder of living.

We should respond with a seriousness that matches the seriousness of the gift. We have each been given a brief span of time in which to mold the raw material of our character into something that might bring joy, healing and inspiration to others. This is the universal human calling: to make ourselves into people who leave a positive legacy that others can draw on to deal with suffering and an example they might use to move themselves beyond their own untutored state.

Given the greatness of the gift and the universal mission it entails, no response but one of sober-minded determination to fulfill the call is suitable. When we respond with anything less, we do a disservice to ourselves and to others, both to our contemporaries and to those who will come after us.

One way we do this disservice is by raising the question, through our unserious behavior if not in speech, about whether life is really a gift at all. When we do this, we teach others to doubt the value of life, to doubt the seriousness of their power, to doubt the gravity of the universal mission in light of the seriousness of evil, darkness and despair.

This is why the wearing of silly hats at the homeschool meeting was such a significant act. Though it may seem trivial, it was significant because in behaving so childishly, the men leading the meeting were committing an act of betrayal. The families gathered there looked to them for guidance and encouragement. Instead, the men in charge showed through their actions that the education of children was not that serious or important a thing, thus influencing the attitudes of their followers and weakening their resolve to make a lasting difference in their children's lives. Being sober-minded is about more than decorum or behaving in a way fit for the occasion. It is about seeing the underlying meaning of an event and conducting one's self in ways to further the universal mission of mankind.

What, then, ought one who lacks sober-mindedness do?

Fortunately, there is much that can be done.

The problem can be approached in two ways, from both ends as it were. First, on the behavioral level, he can attempt to begin taking others more seriously, listening to them and respecting their wishes and boundaries. This alone will begin to accustom him to behaving in ways necessary to the moment rather than being, even in moments that call for seriousness, a frivolous, flighty person.

More than this even, he can work on becoming a person who takes seriously the call to make his person and life a blessing to others. As he examines his unique skills in light of universal difficulty and suffering, specific ways that he can help will present themselves. He can make it his mission to build something positive and lasting. Through doing this, he will begin to take his cues for how to act and what to do not from the trivial, frivolous culture around him, but from the serious mission at his core. As he chooses again and again to live in ways that reinforce and support this mission, he will find his behavior more serious even in fun and expansive times because his life is no longer controlled by a manipulative refusal of objectivity or a lack of charity.

Finally, he can work on increasing his appreciation of the gift of life. By contemplating the mystery of existence daily, he will come to see the enormous wonder of the fact that he is here. His appreciation of all things will grow. His ability to respond to the gift will deepen. His behaviors will no longer be characterized by frivolousness, but by deep joyful purposefulness, by deep meaning.

In the end, this awareness will be a blessing not to him alone, but to all those who encounter him. As he grows more serious, he will not grow more gray and humorless. The opposite will happen. As he grows more serious, others will be drawn to him. They will be pulled into his gravity where he might, if he is fortunate, point them away from childish silliness toward the maturity of wonder and of joy.

14

Frugality

A Great Virtue

IN WENDELL BERRY'S SHORT story "A Half Pint of Old Darling"[1], the author describes a woman as moving from "the great virtue of thriftiness to the much smaller virtue of romantic self-sacrifice," when she decides to save her husband from what she thinks might be incipient alcoholism by drinking the whiskey he has purchased. What could Berry have meant by this line? What makes thriftiness or frugality a great virtue?

To answer that question, we must think clearly about what frugality is and is not. In its casual use, frugality means something like "slow to spend money" or "finding the cheapest way to live." At its extreme we might think of a wealthy miser like Ebenezer Scrooge sitting in his dark, unheated abode consuming his bit of gruel. This is wrong. Whatever Ebenezer Scrooge was, he was not frugal.

Defining Frugal

In its deepest and most expansive definition, frugality means an aversion to waste. But it is not mere aversion with no positive moral precept behind it. Lying behind the aversion to waste in the frugal man's heart is a respect for the world in which he finds himself, and a desire to consume its resources judiciously. He does not want to consume or to destroy more than is reasonable to sustain himself and those he loves.

1. Berry, https://storyoftheweek.loa.org/2018/01/a-half-pint-of-old-darling.html.

This does not mean he lives a spartan life. A frugal man is not necessarily an ascetic. The frugal man does not believe that eschewing all luxury is a compelling moral end in itself. Rather, he is a conscious consumer who weighs and balances his consumption against other considerations. He knows that for every luxury there are costs, not just costs to himself alone but also to others. For every luxury he attains, he knows he must pay. He knows others have paid to make this good available to him. Others have labored. Others have sacrificed. Others have endured hardship so that he might now enjoy whatever pleasure is before him.

But he is not only aware of the costs. A frugal man also knows of the benefits. He knows that through his acquisition of goods, he participates in an economy with the power to lift others out of poverty, a system which can sustain and elevate human life. He knows that with every purchase he makes, people all the way back down its production line profit. He also knows that the profit his purchases generate will be translated into myriad other blessings for people all over the world.

Because he knows we live in a world of costs and benefits, a world of trade-offs, he avoids both the traps of miserliness and spend-thriftiness. Looking at each of these in contrast to frugality will help us better understand the concept.

Miserliness and Frugality

Miserliness differs from frugality in several ways. Chief among these is that miserliness does not acknowledge the complexity of the world and proposes a single answer to all questions of personal finance and resource consumption. The simple answer miserliness offers is :don't spend, don't give, don't invest.

Miserliness seeks to hoard rather than to use resources prudently. Miserliness is focused not on profiting, but on not losing. Rather than investing in profitable activities, and consuming goods wisely, the miser simply grips whatever resources are available to him and clutches them tightly.

After Ebenezer Scrooge, the most famous miser in literature is Silas Marner, the titular character in George Eliot's well-known novel. Marner hoards his gold in a bag near his fireplace. Each night he takes it out and fondles it, reveling in its beauty and in the security and power he believes it represents. His riches represent revenge on the people who have wronged him. In the gleam of the gold, Marner sees not its value alone, but, a reassurance of his value in.

Miserliness, unlike frugality, is rooted in fear and insecurity and the desire for revenge. Misers see the hoarding external wealth as a solution to internal suffering. They imagine that by holding onto money and other forms of wealth, they will increase their security and power enough to escape the pain of their internal struggles.

The futility of this approach is evident. Imagine a person with enough money that even without working, her basic needs would be met. She never need fear homelessness or hunger. She never needs to worry about affording shelter or medicine or new clothes. Even when she has all her basic needs met and enough money to guarantee they will be met for the duration of her life, her inner problems remain. No amount of luxury, no number of fancy gadgets or expensive trips do anything to ameliorate the difficulty inside. Rather than use her financial security to purchase time and aid to remedy the real problem, she continues to believe the problem is lack of wealth and seeks to increase her fortune even more.

This is why miserliness is characterized by a lack of generosity. A person who sees the function of wealth as relieving her inner pain cannot spare a penny to ease the pain of another. When she does give, she does so with resentment. She sees giving to another as a loss to herself. This is because she sees wealth as a tool to be used on a problem it can never fix. She has no realistic or workable plan for her wealth. She is driven instead by the emotional needs her damaged ego creates.

Frugality, in contrast, can give. Frugal people know that money is a tool with limited power, very effective at solving a particular set of problems, totally ineffective at solving others. A shower loofah, for example, is an excellent tool for spreading soap around your body. A miser is like a man who uses a loofah to try to drive a nail. Frugal people know what kinds of tools to use for what kinds of problems.

This is the fundamental difference between frugality and miserliness. Frugality is motivated by a desire to use resources in a wise, not wasteful way. Miserliness does not want to use resources at all save as a bulwark against the inner fear the miser hopes to repress. The frugal person is free to spend and invest as wisdom dictates. He is also free to give. He sees giving as an investment in others, in his community and ultimately in himself. He knows that by giving prudently, he will contribute to projects that benefit all. His aim in all he does with his resources is some sort of profit, and he uses his money as a tool to promote physical, emotional and spiritual growth. The miser, because he seeks to live with his wealth in a static relationship, cannot do this.

Spendthriftiness and Frugality

On the opposite end of the spectrum from miserliness, is the spendthrift. The spendthrift makes no effort to manage his resources outside of searching for the next amusement or pleasure to consume. Where the miser seeks to hoard wealth as a means of salving the ache of inner insecurity and fear, the spendthrift uses his resources to avoid his inner world altogether.

If the miser rejoices in sitting in lonely solitude embracing his gold, the spendthrift uses what wealth he has to ensure he will never be alone. Even if what he seeks to keep him company is things and not people, his attitude toward his possessions is driven by a desire to avoid confronting his inner emptiness.

This pattern is easy to see in our consumerist culture. A culture that regards getting and spending as the essence of life yields a substantial portion of the population who lack depth, who are disconnected from inward realities. In a society like ours, many people have forgotten that meaning is an inward experience, not an external, tangible product that can be bought and sold.

The spendthrift envies the rich because they possess greater purchasing power than he, and are therefore less limited in what distractions they can pursue. His envy increases his internal unhappiness, which in turn ramps up his need to spend and find distractions.

For this reason, a spendthrift might be a very hard worker. His desire to live entirely in the external world of sensation is a strong motivator. He may rely on that motive to power him to work long hours or to push his way into a professional field where high salaries are common. Or he may not. Neither the miser nor the spendthrift need be affluent. It is perfectly possible to be either and to have little money.

What makes a miser or a spendthrift is a matter of internal attitude, not a matter of bank account size. We rarely think this because the habits of a miser make his savings grow and the inclinations of a spendthrift empty his accounts. But an insecure, frightened person who hopes money will take his fear away can indulge that miserly delusion even if he possesses but a coin, and the spendthrift can, thanks to our economy of credit, keep spending long after he has exhausted his resources. He merely borrows from others to keep the party going.

Common Good

A Portrait of Frugality

The frugal person is neither miser nor spendthrift. Rather, he approaches wealth with balance and a realistic assessment both of his needs and of the power of wealth. He knows that living a steady, stable life requires a steady, stable inflow of money and other resources. When he has established this, he tends it well, because he desires it to grow. Managing resources well means directing them toward some purposeful end, an end greater and beyond the self. The frugal man knows that resources are a sort of power and rather than hoard or squander them, he focuses on a conscious goal, an end that merits his investment.

Investment, of course, is neither hoarding nor spending. Where hoarding is the mark of the miser, and profligacy the mark of the spendthrift, wise investment is the mark of the frugal man. Both the miser with his hoard and the spendthrift with his empty pockets are focused on the "right now." Both seek instant relief from their anxieties through their wealth. The frugal man plays the long game.

Unlike both the miser and the spendthrift who are motivated by desires and forces they do not recognize, the frugal person is very conscious of a goal outside herself. She has reflected on her desires. She has considered the possibilities and from them chosen a few toward which she will focus her will, intention and resources. When she uses her money to progress in the direction of these goals, she is making an investment. She has faith that what she puts out will come back to her, if not in the form of finances, then in the form of some less tangible satisfaction.

Her goals also allow her to be disciplined. Without a conscious goal, we do not know what to spend, how much to save, what to buy, what to refrain from buying. We have no basis for individual decisions, because we do not know what we are trying to achieve in the long run. Just as a man who does not know his ultimate destination has no basis for knowing whether to turn right or to turn left at an intersection, so we have no basis for deciding what to do with our resources when we are not dedicated to bringing a specific vision into being.

Thus does it appear that the first step toward becoming frugal is to think. We must select among the many possibilities the world offers some goal toward which we will direct our resources. Because this is so, we see that frugality is not the destination we are aiming at. Frugality is not the end in itself, but rather an approach, a posture, a tool which we may use to help us achieve some worthy goal beyond it.

Frugality

This must be so because many resources, money in particular, have no inherent value. Rather, its value lies in what it makes possible. So, the frugal man must be focused on what good is possible for him to achieve. Having a clear direction makes investment possible. When we have a long-term goal, we can make plans for our and others' long-term good. When we invest resources, we are hoping to get a return on them in the long run. Neither the miser nor the spendthrift invests because neither has a long-term vision.

This is one reason Wendell Berry refers to frugality as a great virtue, because it demands that we look to the future and that we take responsibility not only for ourselves in the present moment, but also for the generations to come. Because frugality springs from our concern for those who come after us, it demands we be drawn out of ourselves. Frugality, in this way, connects us to the future.

Frugality and Contentment

We can now see that frugality is also connected to other virtues we might pursue. This is another reason why it is a great virtue. Frugality is a mark of the responsible person pursuing positive goals he hopes to see realized in the future. Above all, frugality is connected to the virtue of contentment.

Contentment means the willingness and ability to be satisfied with our overall circumstances. To understand contentment, it's helpful to distinguish contentment from complacency. Some people easily get these confused. In fact, some people argue against cultivating contentment on the grounds that being content requires us to accept, at best, mediocrity and, at worst, harm. An emphasis on contentment, they say, means being satisfied with less than the best one can achieve or experience.

None of that is necessarily true. People who say these things are arguing against complacency, not contentment. They're different things. Complacency is rooted in anger. Contentment is rooted in gratitude. Complacent people see the world as having wronged them and vow to get their revenge by ceasing to care about any part of it, including their own welfare. This does not mean they accept their circumstances, not by a long shot. To the contrary, they allow their anger about their circumstances to embitter them.

In the soil of this anger, complacency grows. Through a dynamic similar to the one I discussed in the chapter on discipline, the complacent person takes a passive-aggressive stance toward the world. On one hand, he seeks, through his inaction, to punish the world for the disappointments it has dealt him. In his heart of hearts, he seeks to deprive the world of his participation in it therefore demonstrating to it its many injustices.

Of course, he only punishes himself. Only he suffers from his refusal to act. Instead of acting, he complains. He complains to his friends, his enemies, his mother, to anyone whose attention he can momentarily capture. His complaining is a substitute for doing. His complaints are like pent up steam in a boiler. When he releases his negative energy through complaining, he feels like he has done something. In this way, the complacent person lives a life of illusion. In the tension between his complaining and his passivity, he remains stuck. Eventually, he becomes comfortable in that stuck place and grows indifferent to anything but this unwholesome comfort.

The content person operates from gratitude, not resentment. The content do not resent the fundamental nature of reality. They do not perceive themselves to be fundamentally victims. Rather, they see themselves as beings capable of making positive change, and they embrace their power to bring about new realities in the world.

Frugality and Gratitude

This power is one of the things for which they are consistently grateful. To be content is to regard life itself as something which, rather than being inflicted upon us, is given to us as a blessing. When the starting point of one's worldview is a sense of having been given a gift in spite of merit or desert, contentment become easier to attain. When the initial gift is valued properly, everything else we might attain is extra.

This foundation of gratitude allows the content not to grasp constantly for more, just as it prevents them from slipping into the passivity of the complacent. Rather than viewing life as a relentless battle to accumulate more wealth, more status, more privilege, the content are able to regard whatever they have as enough. They have faith that their needs will be met. The content do not live in perpetual panic. The content are free to rest, to delight unperturbed in the circumstances of life.

This does not mean the content do not strive to meet goals. They do, but are impelled by different motives. Their lives are marked by a different emotional tone from the grasping miser or the oblivious spendthrift. The content strive to achieve from a desire to realize a positive vision, to bring some good thing into the world that was not here before.

Frugality

Though they regard life as a gift, and allow themselves to be happy in their circumstances, they do not simply settle for anything. They do not deny problems or blindly accept injustice. They move forward in a spirit of anticipation and joy. Thus, does the tension between being content and achieving goals resolve. Both are possible simultaneously.

Because the content are directed toward bringing positive goods into the world, they are frugal. It's easy to see why. The content person is driven to achieve some goal, not from fear or panic, but from gratitude for the gift of life and from an earnest desire to bless his neighbors. He seeks to use his resources to move himself toward his goal. And so we arrive again at the essence of frugality. He is repulsed by waste because he sees how what is wasted could have contributed to his effort to bring about the good he is aiming for. He does not hoard because he knows that unused resources contribute nothing to the goal. So, with regard to his resources, he occupies the middle space where each expenditure is weighed against the long-term goal and he spends, saves and invests accordingly.

Moving Toward Mission

The first step toward developing frugality is to think is because the first step toward frugality is developing a sense of meaning, of mission. Without this, the management of our resources, like everything else we do, will be directionless. The first question to be asked when we decide to develop the virtue of frugality is "what am I trying to achieve with my life?"

For many people, this question is far more intimidating than the question of "should I buy this?" The reason is clear. The former demands an assessment of the deepest parts of ourselves, while the latter refers merely to one decision. People find the question of what they are trying to achieve with their lives intimidating for a couple of reasons: first, because they believe the answer is hard to know, and second because the answer is a call to action, a call to change and growth, and thus a challenge to one's courage.

In one sense the answer to "what should I do with my life? What should my mission be?" Is simple because the answer is the same for everyone. For all of us, the simple answer is "become the best version of yourself." Or, to put it another way, "develop into all you were meant to be." As I said earlier, the human being has inside himself a plan for maturity and her goal is to allow that plan to unfold. All of us have an ideal self, a mental version of ourselves that we would like to be in reality. The mission of every human life is to move toward that ideal.

But not every ideal self is the same, and this is where individual differences come into play. Because every ideal self is unique, the path to realizing it will be different for everyone. For one, doing this may involve mastering a musical instrument, for another a science, for another a sport. The point is that we can know our mission in part by honestly looking at the kind of person we know inside we were meant to become. When we have accepted this reality, we will see a course of action necessary to move toward being that person. These actions constitute the individual steps our mission requires us to take.

Many of those steps will be scary. We will have to move out of our comfort zones. This is the second reason why people resist knowing their missions. When we know our mission, we will find that to live it requires a deeper commitment to action, a new level of bravery, a new tolerance for risk. It's easier to deny what we know our ideal selves to be, and to pretend we weren't made for more. It is far easier to move into complacency, to become a miser or a spendthrift than it is to gin up the courage to move in the direction of our ideal selves, of what we were meant to be.

A commitment to moving toward our ideal selves with transform our use of resources. Eventually, we will be compelled to bring our resource use into alignment with the mission we are on. This means we will become frugal. No longer will we hoard our resources as a source of empty comfort. We can now see that this is the path of stymied growth. Miserliness attempts to arrest the process of growth, to find a comfortable spot along the path and to settle there. This attitude we have described as complacency. We can reject it if we can find the courage.

We can also reject the hedonistic approach of the spendthrift. When we know we are on a path to development and fulfillment, we no longer need to escape internal or external realities through distraction and dissipation. We can save, spend and invest in ways that bring us closer to the reality we seek to embody, rather than make constant attempts to avoid it.

All this lies behind the seemingly simple virtue of frugality. Clearly, it means much more than merely being stingy. It, in fact, means the opposite. Stingy people are those disconnected from the joys of life, of giving and of growth. They have closed in on themselves and to open up again, they could do worse than resolve to leave that stinginess behind and become instead happily frugal.

15

Friendliness

A Lonely Age

OURS IS A LONELY time. People are more disconnected, more desperate for connection than ever. Across the Western world, people are struggling with loneliness in a new way. A few years ago, the government of the United Kingdom went so far as to appoint the first government official to deal with this problem, creating the world's first ever minister of loneliness.[1]

The reasons for this are many. Technology, our globalized economy, a relaxing of divorce laws and a hedonistic culture have all worked together to weaken our social bonds. We live now in a web of social relations that are mostly utilitarian and shallow, and while many now assume this is normal, it is not an environment in which human beings flourish.

Friendship Is the Antidote

Friendship is the antidote to our loneliness. We reach out to others seeking to secure the many goods that come with positive and affirming relationships. We look to others for aid and counsel, real-world practical help and for fun. This is completely natural, of course, but our culture has developed in ways that have made this process difficult.

Factors both internal and external to the individual make it tough to make friends these days. External factors include the general mobility of our population and a consumer culture that encourages us to shape our

---

1. John, Tara. https://time.com/5248016/tracey-crouch-uk-loneliness-minister/.

lives not around meaningful relationships, but around ephemeral consumer experiences.

In the fifty years following World War II, Western Culture, and American culture in particular, became increasingly mobile. Though the rate has decreased in recent years, at one point, a significant percentage of American's were moving every year[2]. The reasons for this were many. People moved for jobs. People moved to go to school. People moved away just for adventure. Opportunities, it seemed, abounded for those willing to cut ties and go.

In many ways, it was true. Many of the most mobile among us found success. For a while, leaving family and friends in order to acquire wealth and pleasure in an exotic locale seemed like a good deal. Some however found the things left behind hard to replace. Though the country became littered with disposable apartments and chain restaurants rendering most places indistinguishable from one another, replacing what was unique in the place we left, namely the connections we had with family and friends, showed itself to be much harder than we had anticipated. The result was a population of people who, in spite of their professional success, felt disconnected, adrift and lonely.

While mobility was optional—one could choose to stay or go—the second factor came looking for everyone until there was no escape. Consumer culture blossomed and transformed everything it touched, including our relationships. Whether you lived in a metropolis or in a hamlet, consumer culture came to you.

Consumer culture is a culture in which all institutions are subordinated to the demands of the market and in which traditional cultural practices and artifacts are replaced with consumer goods and popular culture. As consumer culture grew in strength, many people focused both their leisure time and disposable income on buying a pre-packaged consumer experience. A typical Saturday morning might involve driving to the commercial strip in a big city, having lunch in one of the many chain restaurants, spending time buying things at the Mall, seeing a movie and then having another restaurant meal before driving home to watch television including the many commercials showing you consumer experiences that still awaited you.

Of course, people didn't do these things alone, but together. Where earlier generations forged friendships in the grind of daily life at a time when daily life required many more chores than it does now, we form friendships

---

2. White, https://www.moving.com/tips/us-moving-statistics-for-2019/.

around what we consume. Liking the same consumer and pop culture goods has become a prerequisite for friendship among modern people.

Rather than becoming friends based on shared values or an ability to offer one another mutual aid in difficult times, modern people become friends because they both love Star Wars. A common interest in some pop culture phenomenon has become the basis for getting to know one another more deeply. More importantly, popular consumer culture is now the basis for self-understanding as many people began to draw their identities from the pop culture items they consume. Do you like hard rock and beer? Well, that tells you what sort of person you are. You are very different from your neighbor because she only listens to emo and smokes clove cigarettes. As consumer culture has progressed, people inside it begin to identify themselves with the marketing segment into which they have been sorted.

The complications of modern friendship have internal dimensions as well, dimensions of the soul and mind. As people began to identify themselves as consumers of a particular set of goods, options for travel and communications were increasing. People were increasingly empowered to spend more of their time with others whose consumer identities were like their own. Eventually, with the rise of the Internet, the ability to dwell in a bubble in which everyone shared your interests, assumptions and biases was almost total.

Now instead of friendships demanding growth, acceptance and negotiation, they increasingly demanded intense signaling of loyalty to the group and the things that defined its members' identity. Friendship became less a force drawing one out of oneself and more about reflecting images of one another back in a kind of mutual narcissistic dance.

At the same time, our hedonistic consumer culture has changed the definition of friendship and the expectations people hold of it. In a culture built around the consumption of pleasurable experiences, most people think a friend is someone you pursue pleasurable experiences with, someone you eat with at restaurants, someone you see movies with, someone you go to concerts with. Deeper understandings of friendships have given way; the entire psychological infrastructure of our culture supports and approves only this one.

Other models of friendship are rare now. This has not always been the case, in part, because different social structures condition different sorts of friendships. In Flora Thompson's recounting of growing up in a pre-industrial English village, she talks at length about the way village life naturally encouraged relationships that, rather than being built around consumer experiences, were simply part of the warp and woof of everyday life.³

In one section she talks extensively about how the men of the village would work together in the fields during the day and then spend time together in the pub each evening. The women were equally in each others' company daily. She details how they would be in and out of each others' homes often during the day either to help with chores or just to break the monotony with a chat. Such a culture gives rise to a very different understanding of friendship from the one we experience in the globalized, digitized post-war West.

The result of this shift has been a tremendous and unique kind of loneliness. Some people have always been lonely, but never before has that loneliness been constituted in precisely this way. Modern loneliness is like nothing that has come before.

Pushing Back against the Age

The solution is to push back where we can and to try, at least in our personal lives, to create an atmosphere where friendships can take root and at a deeper level. If that is to happen, we must be intentional about cultivating some specific practices and attitudes. We must cultivate the virtue of friendliness.

This means, first, we must try to be the kind of person with whom others would want to be friends. Naturally, this means cultivating all the virtues we discussed so far in this book, but it means more than that too. It means that we first seek to know why we want to have friends. We must make sure our understanding of friendship is rooted in something more than the simple consumption of consumer experiences. If we want to find friends, we must know what we are looking for.

If friendships are not to be rooted in consumption, in what should they be rooted? Well, different levels of relationship are rooted in different places. Think of them as different kinds of plants whose roots each go to a different depth in the soil. Just like these plants, different relationships will be rooted at different levels in our lives. Some will have deep roots and some shallow. This is fine since even plants with shallow roots can yield beautiful flowers.

3. Thompson, *Lark Rise to Candleford: A Trilogy*, 118–19

Friendliness

Levels of Relationship

The first level will be relationships rooted in accident: relationships with people we happen to work with, happen to pass in the hallway of our apartment building or with whom we happen to live on the same street. We never consciously intended to be near these people. Life simply brought us into proximity through the ever-shifting circumstances of history. These relationships will be shallow by virtue of their origin. All relationships are shallow when they begin, but all have the potential to become more if conditions are right. This situation differs from the kind of shallowness mentioned above. Consumer friendships are not shallow merely because of their origin, but because of their nature. They do not have the potential to grow deep under any circumstances.

None of this means we don't have an opportunity to practice the virtue of friendliness in even transient situations. We should not devalue even these relationships simply because they are fleeting or restricted. Even in brief encounters, we can bring light and good cheer to those we encounter. Our smile is often the best way to do this. Do not underestimate the power of a friendly smile. Human beings are very sensitive creatures and even something as seemingly insignificant as a routine smile can shape our feelings and influence our decision making.

Another reason to value these relationships is that from among them arise relationships with the capacity for more. No one can tell by looking at the flower how deep the roots may go.

The next level of friendship is rooted in common interests. By practicing friendliness at the level of passing acquaintance, we open the door to discovering commonalities between ourselves and others. When we do, the potential for greater connection opens up. These common interests may be anything. Yes, even pop culture and consumer enthusiasms. The problem I was pointing out earlier wasn't that people share an interest in popular culture; the problem is that they build their relationships exclusively around these, and therefore have no relationships with deep roots.

Relationships at this level can, in spite of their relatively shallow roots, be pleasant and enjoyable. We might find that our common interests open the door to many great experiences that eventually become cherished memories. By joining with others to pursue things that delight or elevate us, we can intensify the positive effects of our hobbies and passions while creating rewarding bonds with others.

From this level of friendship, if we are fortunate, we might find yet some relationships whose roots go to a level deeper still. These are people with whom we share not merely common interests, but common values as well. These are the people with whom we can cultivate a deeper connection, people who not only enjoy the same things we do, but whose points of view and understanding of life mirror our own. These are the people whom we can accurately and fully call friends. Because of our shared connection built around both interests and values, we will have a sense of being in the midst of life together, will have a sense that in the midst of turmoil and trouble these people are on our side. We trust these people.

Out of these people we sometimes find those with whom our friendships can reach the deepest level. These are people with whom we share both interests, values and a deep sense of mission. With these people the sense of shared values goes to the very core of our being. We not only are interested in the same things, and share similar values, we also want the same things. We want reality to be shaped in the same way, we want to achieve the same goals and are able to help one another achieve these.

When we find ourselves with people with whom we share the same mission, we have found ourselves the deepest kind of friends. We are bound not merely by accident or passing shared amusement, by a sense of being co-workers laboring toward the same mission. This makes the bond between us as strong as possible. With these people we have a sense of being bound together by something more than preference, something deep, mystical and inescapable.

A fulfilling and peaceful life requires relationships at all these levels. It's easy to think, especially when we are young, that we need many, many friendships and that all of them should be deep and intense. As we age, we see that the soil of our lives can only hold so many plants of that nature and we become grateful for the riches of the many kinds of relationships that are available to us.

But, what about people who simply don't have these kinds of relationships? Or perhaps any of the kinds of relationships I have described here? What should those people do? The answer is simple, those people should work to cultivate the virtue of friendliness, the habit of being the kind of friend they are seeking.

Friendliness

Finding Friends

This is not to say that lonely people are entirely to blame for their loneliness. As we have seen, many cultural factors come into play in our modern loneliness, but this should not discourage us from making the most of our influence and control in realms where we can make a difference.

Finding friends and developing relationships is one of the areas where we have quite a bit of sway. So, the first thing a lonely person should do is begin attending to the first level of relationships and focus on finding persons who might move to the second level. This can be a daunting assignment for those whose loneliness is intense. It's not uncommon for very lonely people to rush this stage. This desire, however, can undermine the process, extending the period of loneliness even further.

Failing to allow this process the full time it requires leads to three mistakes. First, it discourages taking this stage with the requisite seriousness. Because lonely people are motivated by a desire to satisfy an intense need, it's easy for them to conclude that this stage, because it does not make their pain go away, can be neglected. The solution to this is to force oneself to go slowly as the process rolls on.

Second, lonely people often fail to discriminate adequately. Their loneliness obscures their ability to sort through their acquaintances to truly see who would make a good friend. The result is a lot of frustration borne of failed attempts at developing relationships with people for whom they are not suited. Their impatience leads to a lot of awkwardness and, in some cases, hurt feelings. To avoid this, the lonely person must cultivate enough self-possession to recognize who truly shares their interests and who is merely in proximity to them via some accident of space and time.

The final mistake people tend to make in this stage is to try to rush to inappropriate levels of intimacy. The rush to intimacy often earns them the label "needy" or "desperate." To avoid this, lonely people don't have to hide their loneliness, but should instead focus on what they have to give rather than on having their loneliness salved. The greater the focus on bringing value to others, the less internal pressure to get close too quickly.

The skills described here: self-control, a willingness to focus on providing value, a clear sense of who is well-suited for a developing friendship, are all part of the virtue of friendliness. It should be easy to see now the dilemma in which the lonely find themselves. No one can cure his loneliness without being friendly, but intense loneliness, especially when it unconsciously drives our behavior, hinders our ability to be friendly.

The only way out of this quandary is to resolve to cultivate friendliness no matter what, to focus on virtue instead of our feelings. To increase our chances of success, we can begin by preparing the proper soil. That proper soil means having a right approach to relationships, a healthy understanding of other people's role in our lives.

I have already mentioned that extreme loneliness can cause people to behave in ways that others find off-putting. Having the right mindset can keep this situation from developing. To think rightly, we must understand that our level of popularity or the number of connections we enjoy is not an indication of out worth.

It is very easy to believe that our worth and value is determined by what others reflect back to us. This is not the case. Others' behaviors are often not about us at all. When we imagine their behaviors toward us are reflections of our worth, we mistake what is actually a reflection of their values, beliefs and self-image for a reflection of us. We engage in a fundamental boundary confusion. We do not know who in this situation is who.

Understanding our Inherent Worth

To counter this, we can choose to understand ourselves as beings with inherent worth that can neither increase nor decrease based upon others' ideas about us. When we see that we have this kind of inherent worth and are able to unhook ourselves from the roller coaster of seeking others approval, our vision of relationships is free to transform into something healthier, something more capable of producing good results. And we are more free to cultivate friendliness.

Once we have settled the matter of our worth, we can be proactive instead of reactive in our approach to relationships. When we do not see ourselves as having inherent worth, we look to others to reassure us of our value. We cannot approach others from anything but a position of need. When we understand our inherent value, we can approach others determined to share that value.

This allows us to begin cultivating the friendly virtues of confidence and good will. When we believe we have something positive to offer others, this becomes the center of our interactions. Instead of needing others to give us something, we are free to approach them with the desire to share what we have. We look for ways to elevate and uplift others.

Friendliness

On the first level of friendship described above, this may be as simple as sharing a smile or a brief hello. Positive actions, even small ones, send signals of warmth and accessibility. These will resonate with some of those we encounter, and this will open a door to new levels of relationship. The strategy of offering others what we have that is of value is workable across all the levels of intimacy. When we begin to move to new levels, we find we have the opportunity to add value to the lives of others at ever-deeper levels and in more powerful ways.

When we focus on offering others something of value, we can begin to respect their freedom. We no longer need to try to control them because we have a sense that our value is independent of their response to us. Respecting others and their freedom to choose is one aspect of friendliness. When we allow others the freedom to choose whether they are interested in what we have to offer, we communicate to them that they matter and we communicate the respect we feel and this, in turn, makes our relationships more viable.

Eventually, we come to see that if we want more friends, the solution is not to control or manipulate others, but to increase what we have to offer. The advantage of this approach is that it keeps the power in our hands. Rather than obsessing over what others think of us, we can get obsessed with the good we offer others. This desire to do good for others is the essence of friendliness.

When we practice increasing what we have to offer others long enough, we find we no longer need to go looking for friends because they come to us. This is the essence of non-loneliness, not having a bunch of friends, but knowing deep inside that we will always have an abundance of connections because others flourish when connected with us. It turns out that loneliness is, in part, about what we think of ourselves just as much as it is about what others think of us.

This is what the virtue of friendliness is in the end, a series of choices that increase our value and trustworthiness to a level that yields connections with others so strong we still feel them even when the other is physically absent. Our virtue, more than making us popular, connects is in ways no separation can ever damage. Virtue, in the end, more than popularity is what keeps us in the best company.

16

Domesticity

Our Anti-Home Mindset

WE ARE RAISED TO go away. From the time we are children in American culture, we labor under the assumption that at some point, it will be time for us to turn our backs on our childhoods and go. We are taught to think our best possible future lies out there somewhere, somewhere away from the place we grew up and the people with whom we grew up. Few of us know what future we are aiming at, we only believe that somehow it lies far away.

This attitude is only one expression of the general disdain in which our culture holds the home. Home is the place where nothing happens. Home is the place we come to sleep when we have exhausted ourselves with work and play. The best thing we can do with our homes is to leave them.

We associate the home with drudgery, with retreat, even with a type of surrender. Home is for losers. Consider the common associations with the word "homebody." This word conjures up more than the simple idea of someone who prefers to stay home. It brings with it the idea that this person is dowdy and suffers from either painful shyness or bitter defensiveness. If such things were not true, we wonder, why would these people prefer to stay home? The point is that we do not view home and those who prefer it in a positive light.

Because we are taught that success lies away from home, we naturally assume those who stick close are losers. Indeed, many of us unconsciously measure the success of another by how little he is required to be at home. We think the successful man is the one who travels much, who spends his days rushing about in the company of strangers, doing work that benefits distant, remote entities neither he nor we can name.

This mindset proves very profitable for those at the top. "Away from home" is where most buying and selling happens. Keeping us out of the home means keeping us engaged in the market. Keeping us engaged in the market means keeping the money flowing from our pockets to theirs.

That we are all raised to assume that we will find our greatest fulfillments in the world of work and not at home is simply another way of saying we are raised to prioritize the profits of others over our own peace and independence. When we shift these assumptions, we empower ourselves. In many instances, "home" is just a symbol for our own lives, for the needs and wants that lie beneath the programming we have been subjected to and behind the facade we have been persuaded to accept as real.

Reclaiming Home

To reclaim home and therefore our lives, we must think more deeply about what the home is. The home is much more than merely a place where we eat, sleep and watch television. The home is the seat of our real life. Ideally, it is here that we are free from the strictures of the marketplace, and here that we employ that freedom to grow toward the person we know in our hearts we ought to be. At home, we cultivate virtue. While, of course, the marketplace calls upon us to practice virtue as well, home is the place where we can be nurtured into new virtues or into new levels of the virtues we already possess.

At home, the measure of value is different or, at least, should be. At home we are valued at least as much for who we are as for what we produce. This acceptance apart from our performance forms a foundation for our moral growth. Here at home we can experiment, we can try and fail without fear. It is at home that we get better.

Most homes do not measure up to this ideal. For many, home falls far short of what "ought" to be. The real source of acceptance and freedom for these people lies elsewhere. This inhibits the growth process. At their worst, these situations not only inhibit growth, they pervert it. Instead of simply growing at a slower pace, the situation in our homes deforms us and causes us to grow into forms we were never intended to bear.

The fact that home is sometimes an uncomfortable place does not negate the fact that for all of us, the home Is primary. None of us longs to spend his days at a job doing work we find meaningless. We'd rather be somewhere else. We would rather inhabit a different frame of values. We would rather be at peace. We would rather be at leisure. A more humane set of values characterize our home. Even if the place where we grew up was no good, even if every member of our family is irredeemably toxic, we still desire to dwell in a place where our moments are characterized by these domestic categories of value. The part of our life where we experience acceptance, peace and freedom will always matter more to us than that part where our value is contingent upon our production, where we must engage the rough and tumble world. Wherever we experience peace, freedom, acceptance and leisure is our home. And because the things we experience at home are always more important to us than the things we experience in the world of the market, the home is always primary in our affections.

Home is a physical place, but more than that too. Home is a set of conditions, a certain way things are. These conditions are physical, relational and emotional.

We all have physical needs. We need to eat, for one. We need to rest. We need to be sheltered from the elements. Home is the place that nourishes our physical selves. At home, we have those things that bring us physical comfort. We have favorite snacks stored in a cabinet. We have that pair of sweatpants we change into every day when we return from work. We have a favorite blanket we spread over ourselves when we retire for the evening. Home is a place where we keep the things we need to nourish and comfort the body. At home, we should not know real deprivation. Home should not be cold, or rigid or rough. These characteristics belong to non-home places: to the market or to the wilderness.

Our relationships at home should be just as warm and just as nourishing. In these, we should find reassurance that we are not alone in our struggles. Here we find companionship, guidance and belonging. We should know that when we come home, whoever else is there is on our side. At home, as opposed to in the marketplace, our interests are one with those around us. What's good for one is good for all. At the heart of the home is not individual will, but an experience of unity that sustains us when we are away.

These factors contribute to the inner emotional conditions a home requires. At home, we should be comforted and comfortable. Home ought to be neither an anxious nor a frightful place, but a place of serenity and joy. Perhaps more than anything else, the inner sense of peace and freedom we feel at home defines it for us. When we are at home, we can do what we like, follow our own agendas without fear. We can allow our muscles to soften. We can breathe more deeply. Life moves more slowly when we are at home. Home gives us the opportunity to appreciate life and its many blessings by affording us time to reflect on them. A well-functioning home fills us with gratitude.

The Necessity of Domesticity

Again, these are ideals. Some people's dwellings cannot, by these standards, be called home. Others have some measure of these but fall far short of the mark in every category. Others are closer, to the ideal but no one's home meets these ideals perfectly. Because we can know the ideal, we can see the ways in which our homes fall short of them. This shortfall requires, then, that we cultivate virtue that makes the place we dwell more ideal.

The central virtue that allows this is domesticity. By cultivating domesticity, we focus on our homes, we create an oasis for ourselves and others in the chaotic world. We strive to develop a small place that satisfies us at the physical, relational and emotional levels. We create our domain, one we rule for and by ourselves.

Domesticity requires activities that move us forward on each of the three levels mentioned above. Domestic virtues, for example, express themselves in the physical aspects of our home. Many years ago, near the end of college and just after, I shared an apartment with another man about my age. Neither of us had much domestic virtue. The apartment was essentially a shell to contain our stuff, a place to watch television and to sleep. Once in a while, we would go on a big cleaning spree and bring everything up to an acceptable level of order and then let household duties slide until we entered into the next big cleaning rush.

This pattern was not an expression of domestic virtue because we were not doing what was required to provide ourselves with a physically nourishing atmosphere. We never ate at home, living essentially on fast food during those years. To begin developing our domestic virtues, we would have had to do many things differently.

Developing domestic virtue does not mean having a pristine home or living perpetually in a magazine photograph of a gorgeous room. Developing domestic virtue means taking responsibility to develop yourself by creating environments in which the whole person is more likely to grow. Domestic virtue is an expression of the human ability to direct our own growth.

The chief expression of this virtue in the physical realm is cleanliness. Cleanliness does not mean spotlessness, but an unwillingness to bring one's living space up to a level of basic sanitation indicates a lack of domestic virtue. A basic threshold of cleanliness is attainable by most people.

Of course, people have varying understandings of what constitutes "clean." My purpose here is not to prescribe some standard which must be met in order to demonstrate domestic virtue. Because people's understanding of what a clean home is varies widely, the best we can say is that the standard we must defend is one which allows the human being to flourish.

No one flourishes when food is rotting on the kitchen counter and pets are defecating on the floor. Situations like this are far from what is necessary for their inhabitants' health. Almost everyone would agree that a standard which says that basic hygiene must be valued is reasonable. When seeking to define this standard more fully however. There are other factors we can consider other than basic hygiene.

Once we get beyond basic sanitation however, our ability to say with definite clarity what is and is not acceptable weakens. People must be free to decide what their homes will be like or we risk undermining the freedom that defines the sense of home. Since our ability to offer prescriptive directives is hindered once we move beyond basic sanitation, let me simply lay out a few principles to consider when thinking about our homes' physical condition.

The first is comfort. When we want to be in a comfortable environment, few of us think of a place that is chaotic. Living in a field of visual and physical chaos is not comforting. Living in a home in need of major repairs is equally unappealing. It's hard to be comfortable in winter when the windows won't close or in summer when they won't open.

Creating a more comfortable environment means taking the responsibility to keep things in good enough order. Because people have varying levels of tolerance for discomfort and because we calculate comfort differently, we must all cultivate good judgement and honestly assess whether we are neglecting domestic duties which, were they adequately discharged, would make us a lot more comfortable.

Efficiency is another principle to keep in mind. Human flourishing happens best when we are not living in an environment that unduly slows us down or hinders our movements. Homes characterized by clutter to the point where stacks of stuff impede movement, where needed objects cannot be easily located or where we cannot rest comfortably without moving piles from the bed to the floor are not efficient. In these cases, our mismanaged environment requires time we could invest to better ends elsewhere. Although we cannot arrive at a perfect universal definition of cleanliness, we can agree our environments should allow us to use our time the we way we desire rather than using it to rearrange our clutter.

Finally, we must cultivate some measure of beauty in our homes. Beauty uplifts and elevates us. Some people naturally emphasize this value more than others. Some will devote their time and energy to filling their home with beautiful objects perfectly arranged. It is not necessary that everyone do this. Still, it is important to think about how we might make our homes more than utilitarian sleeping boxes. The more beauty and order we bring to our homes the more they will reflect back to us the persons we desire to become and thus contribute to our flourishing.

Domestic virtue can make itself seen on the relational level as well. When we cultivate good relationships with those with whom we live, we display this aspect of domestic virtue. We can break domestic virtue in this arena into two components consideration and hospitality.

Those with whom we live will always differ from us. Some will value order more highly, some will value freedom. Still others will bring a different set of emphases into the mix. Differing values lead to conflict.

Book after book has been written about how to create peaceful relationships. I need not explore that question in depth here except to say that in a home all people living there must consider the needs and wants of others. We each must be, in this sense, considerate.

This does not mean that one person's values must dominate. It means that some workable arrangement must be found that takes into account the various agendas and desires of all members of the household. They can each help this to happen simply by considering how our decisions might impact all the others in the home. This is the first step to peaceful relations: thinking of one another.

Next, we must enter into the negotiations stage in which we resolve the tensions that arise when people live together. The key to success here is to approach the negotiations with a conviction that everyone involved has legitimate desires and equally legitimate understanding of what makes a home a place of freedom and joy. Only from that basis can a new synthesis emerge.

Our level of domestic virtue affects more than merely those with whom we live. Just as we call the practice of domestic virtue with those with whom we dwell "consideration," so we call this same virtue when aimed outward toward friends or strangers "hospitality."

Hospitality focuses on creating a public outreach of the private home. Hospitality is the recognition that those who dwell together find the fullest expression of their small community in the act of inviting others in. When a community of those sharing a home reaches out to others, they once again mirror a plant in healthy soil and sunshine. Their community reaches out toward the wider world and enlarges. Without some sort of hospitality practice, people sharing a home tend to devolve, to stymie. Without a commitment to hospitality, families sharing a home become merely individuals sharing a house.

Hospitality means orienting one's home around something other than private comfort and power. Private comfort and power are important, but when exercised exclusively toward self-oriented ends, they fail to realize their fullest possibilities.

Fuller possibilities come into view when we share the gifts of our domestic arrangements with others. Then, the comfort we have created and the power we enjoy can be put to even higher ends. When we practice hospitality, we welcome one deprived of these things, whether by tragedy or travel, to share ours. As with most things related to virtue, we find that this willingness doubles rather than halves our joy.

Our culture erects many obstacles to hospitality. One is the notion of privacy. Moderns, despite how much we share on social media, are in many ways very private people. Our privacy is not so much born from a profound sense that some parts of ourselves and our lives are sacred and should therefore be shielded from public gaze. Rather, our privacy is born from the conviction that what we possess is ours and ours alone. Sharing, we feel, is in some sense losing.

Thus, we encounter skepticism about the practice of hospitality. Some may be reluctant to offer to bring another into their homes because they fear dropping the right to claim exclusive ownership, or at least exclusive use, of their things. Some people have an innate feeling that their space is being invaded even when they themselves have invited the other in.

Conversely, some people are hesitant to accept offers of hospitality for fear of being perceived as an intruder. Some people feel this even when they have been graciously invited multiple times to come, sit and stay. They simply cannot. These people struggle to believe the invitation is sincere. Their refusal of hospitality communicates a distrust of the one offering it, an assumption that they do not mean what they say.

As with everything in this chapter, it is impossible to lay down ironclad prescriptive rules about hospitality. No one can tell you whom you should invite into your home or when, much less can anyone tell you why you should invite some in and not others. These are boundaries you alone can erect. The principle is the point. We grow when we share. What to share and with whom are decisions you must make for yourself.

Finally, we ought to exercise the domestic virtues in a way that makes our homes an emotionally satisfying place. Our home should not be a place where we feel frazzled or distressed. Home is meant to be a refuge. Whether it is or not largely depends on how and to what degree we exercise the domestic virtues.

It should be clear that if we neglect to make our homes a clean and well-ordered space, we will feel anxious. If we fail to bring some measure of comfort or beauty to our environment, we will feel unsettled and restless. We will find ourselves wanting to be somewhere other than at home.

Just as our homes can fail to be emotionally satisfying when we fail to make them comfortable and well-ordered, they will feel emotionally unsatisfying if we neglect their relational aspects. The more harmony we establish in our home, the more emotionally settled we will feel there.

Developing an emotionally satisfying home requires a sensitivity to our own souls, to our desires and preferences as well as to virtue. In fact, it could be said that learning to honor our legitimate inner impulses and to build spaces that reflect and respond to them is a virtue of its own. While the principles of domestic virtue are universal, each person's home must reflect the individual inhabitants' personalities. Because each of us has somewhat varying tastes and emotional needs, what satisfies us will vary as well.

Domesticity and Satisfaction

In the end, satisfaction is what we seek through the creation of a home. When we build for ourselves a place that restores us, that tells us who we are and reminds us of that to which we aspire, we cannot help but develop a deeper and more lasting sense of satisfaction. Knowing we have well-ordered place in the world, a haven in the chaos, satisfies something in the human soul that has gone long neglected in the modern world.

When we look at the lack of domestic virtue most people evince, it is not surprising that the anti-home narrative promoted by our culture would gain such traction. When we have not made the necessary efforts to transform our homes from utilitarian storage sheds into environments that calm and satisfy us, then a story that tells us our deepest satisfaction lies beyond those walls makes more sense. Through the exercise of these domestic virtues, we can reverse this narrative, if not in the culture at large, then certainly in our personal lives.

As we do this, our homes become places that empower us to see through the conventions of our culture and to look more deeply into the truth. This process leads to the ultimate reward for exercising domestic virtues: positive changes in our inner world. When we invest in our homes, we create a backdrop against which meaning is experienced and communicated.

Thus does the reality of our home lift us into new realms of understanding and awareness. When we surround ourselves with a calm, well-ordered environment that envelopes us in meaning, we can reach out from this steady base. We find we are able to move more confidently in the world, that we are more able to extend ourselves to neighbors and strangers, that we are more ready to explore the world simply because we have a place to stay put.

17

Curiosity

Curiosity Constrained

I SPENT A LONG time teaching college, or trying to at least. Most students desired to learn nothing. More often than not, they were in the class because it was a requirement for their major and having a major is a requirement for getting a degree, and a degree, they believed, is a requirement for getting a job.

For the vast majority of college students, their educations are exercises in hoop-jumping rather than a passionate engagement with the world. Many college students learn next to nothing. This reality was born out in the recent past by a study showing most college students learn nothing in their first three years. A few years ago, The Atlantic magazine reported on a study showing that 45 percent of college student had made no significant gains in learning in the first two years[1]. If my experience is a reliable indicator, learning doesn't go up much in the last two, either.

The state of our college students is a testament to our society's general lack of curiosity. In the years I spent teaching hundreds of students, precisely two came to my office to ask questions. That was the extent of the curiosity I encountered. The dearth of curiosity came out in other ways as well. Once, I was showing a class a short film that contained a scene of two men speaking Irish. Two female students near the front of the room mocked the men and laughed. I am certain neither even knew the Irish

---

1. Hayden, https://www.theatlantic.com/culture/archive/2011/01/study-says-college-students-don-t-learn-very-much/342624/.

had a language. I am certain neither had ever heard it spoken. I am certain neither had any interest in finding out what this strange language might be.

These experiences illustrate a wider problem. Across the board in our society, from children to college students to senior citizens, we live now with a near total lack of curiosity. We rarely wonder, even more rarely ponder. When we talk, we ask fewer questions than we make claims.

The Costs of Incurious Attitudes

Incurious attitudes lead to circumscribed and narrow lives. When we cease to be curious, we cease to engage the world. Curiosity is a virtue when it drives us out of our small, confined arenas of comfort and into the unknown. Curiosity is a virtue when it leads us to expand ourselves and to grow. It is this kind of curiosity which was so painfully absent in my students. Perhaps this lack is more noticeable in college students since they spend so much time in institutions purported to be devoted to the pursuit of knowledge, but the same lack is apparent in people from all segments of our society.

The reasons for this are many, and before I explore some of them, let me offer a caveat. Some might rightly point out that much damaging and immoral behavior can be ascribed to curiosity. It's true that curiosity can lead people to do bad things. Yes, people pursue ideas and activities they ought not because of their desire to know. That does not mean that the urge to know is bad, only that it needs to be managed. Curiosity does not stand alone, but in order to achieve its purpose of aiding our growth, it must be teamed with other virtues like self-restraint and moderation.

Curiosity about negative and destructive experiences tends to lead to its own undermining. Curiosity about drugs and their effects, for example, tends to be counter-productive. People whose drug use progresses from a mere curious dalliance to full-blown addiction destroy their ability to be curious. To the degree that curiosity is a function of the mind, anything which weakens our minds undermines our ability to practice curiosity. To the degree that curiosity is a function of the soul, anything which limits, damages or restricts our souls undermines our ability to practice curiosity. The virtuous practice of curiosity means practicing it in a sustainable way, and that means allowing it to lead us into fields of endeavor that do not weaken or undermine us or our functioning.

Obstacles to Curiosity

So, what then is curiosity? Ultimately, curiosity is a desire to know and experience that emerges from the basic joy we take in life. Curiosity flows from a basic apprehension of life's inherent goodness. When we realize that life has come to us as a gift, we have a natural desire to explore that gift, to see what it can do, to know and experience it fully. That natural desire is curiosity.

Negative attitudes about life dampen our curiosity. Anger and resentment close us in upon ourselves. They focus us exclusively on our pain or on the parts of the world we don't like. This focus drives our curiosity underground, smothers our desire to know and to experience more.

Arrogance can do the same. As with my students who laughed at the sounds of Irish, the arrogant have no curiosity because they assume everything important to know is already in their realm of experience. Their smug approach to the world privileges all their prior experience as being better than all new experience.

The incurious view people with high levels of curiosity as being, at best, strange. They tend to view the curious as people who are caught up in trivial, arcane matters while they are concerned with "the real world." They write curious people off as irrelevant time-wasters. They take their own provincial perspectives as normative and react poorly when someone challenges them.

The arrogant in particular revile curiosity because curiosity requires humility. Curiosity implies a limit to our current knowledge before which we must be humble. This offends the arrogant because it implies that important things exist outside of their current purview, that important things exist with which they have no contact. It implies that some people know more than they. This fills the arrogant with shame. Rather than accept these realities with joy and moving into the world by expanding their knowledge of it, the arrogant castigate the curious for being "weird."

Moreover, curiosity implies reverence and arrogance reveres nothing but itself. When we are curious about another person or about some aspect of the world, we are motivated to stand before it with a measure of awe. We relate to it as a newcomer, a stranger. In its strangeness, we meet our limits. Here is a place we have never been before. Here is someone we have not encountered. Here is a new idea. All these things bring us to the edge of experience, to our limits. The arrogant cannot be reverent because they cannot tolerate the notion of limits.

Arrogant people do not grow. Curious people do because curiosity compels us forward. Curious people are always encountering the new. Even if a curious person is eagerly studying the past, he encounters the new there daily. Every time he discovers a previously unknown fact about the past, every time he stumbles onto some new insight which transforms his understanding, he encounters something that is, to him, new.

The Benefits of Curiosity

Curious people love the new. They know that in encountering it, they expand themselves. They know this because they have cultivated the habit of encountering the new, again and again. More often than not, when they have the option to try something new, they go for it. Through this process, they become comfortable with newness being a regular part of life. Whether in the form of experiences, relationships or ideas, curious people are open to what they have never before encountered.

This attitude can be difficult to cultivate because human beings love patterns. Our ability to recognize patterns help us to make sense of our environment. Our ability to create patterns helps us to order our environment and to communicate and organize with others. Patterns and our adherence to them make us feel safe and comfortable in what would otherwise be a hostile and confusing world.

All of this is good. The trouble comes when we rely so heavily on our patterns that we begin to travel through life on autopilot. We can rely on our patterns so much that daily life ceases to demand our awareness. Our reliance on patterns can, in this sense, put us to sleep. A reliance on well-worn patterns can make us so comfortable that we begin to fear much that is outside our regular patterns. And so, what began as a helpful tool for getting along in the world becomes a prison.

Curiosity helps us resist this imprisonment. Like everyone else, curious people desire comfort and safety. But through their cultivation of curiosity, they achieve a balance between the familiar and the new, between what comforts and what challenges. The end result is a life that has a vital mix of the elements necessary for growth. Growing people establish enough safety and comfort for themselves that they have a secure foundation from which to seek the new, but not so much that they are lulled into a mental and spiritual stupor.

Curiosity

Finding new experiences is easy. Literally anything you've never done before is a new experience. A new experience doesn't need to require money, much effort or expense. You can have a new experience without leaving the couch. When you stop scrolling through the cable channels and settle on something you've never watched before, you're giving yourself a new experience. You can have a new experience by switching brands of toothpaste or walking around the block in the opposite direction.

Any of these things can be a new experience, but it pays to be more intentional about trying new things. Slightly more adventurous than the examples above would be things like ordering a new item from the menu at your favorite restaurant or, a little more boldly, going to a new restaurant altogether. Maybe you buy and wear a piece of clothing in a color or style you aren't accustomed to. Maybe you risk cracking a joke in your normally boring weekly meeting at work.

Travel might be the way we generate the most intense new experiences. When we go somewhere outside the region we normally inhabit, we put ourselves in a position where every experience is in some sense new. When you travel, even if you've flown in airplanes a thousand times, you likely have never flown in that specific plane, on that specific route, on that specific date. Even familiar activities take on a bit of strangeness when you travel. If you go far enough, you will find that even the language is different. At that point, even the names of things become a new experience. You are swimming in the novel. New things surround you. Travel, because it removes us from our daily patterns, forces us into a new level of awareness. This is one reason so many people like it.

Curiosity and Risk

The down side of this process is that travel, like all new experiences, involves risk. When you allow your curiosity to open you to a new experience, you naturally accept some measure of risk. Even tiny new experiences harbor some risk. If you stop your channel surfing on a program you've never watched before, you might get bored or worse, you might see or hear something that disturbs you. The taste of a new brand of toothpaste might gross you out. The joke you try making at that meeting might fall flat. People might mock that new shirt you wear. If you go on a trip, you might get lost. You might embarrass yourself. You might have to ask for help.

The level of tension and anxiety we feel about trying new things is likely to increase when we move from creating new experiences to embracing new relationships. However when we instigate new experiences, we remain largely in control of what happens. If we don't like the new television program we have settled on, we can change the channel. If we decide our new shirt is not flattering, we don't have to wear it. Even trips abroad can be ended and we can come home to cocoon.

Relationships involve a somewhat lowered capacity for control. Relationships introduce a new element of unpredictability into the mix. If we are curious about another person, we must learn how to navigate the conversations necessary to satisfy that curiosity. When we are seeking new experience alone, we have the luxury of remaining at least somewhat passive. Pursuing relationships intentionally requires greater effort. We must initiate contact, must learn to read the signals about whether further contact is desired, must be honest with ourselves about who the other actually is, must separate the real other from the one we imagined. We must also be curious enough to look at how this new relationship is influencing us. The waters here are more difficult to navigate.

And yet, expanding our network of relationships is a chief source of joy in human life. By allowing our curiosity to drive us toward others, we escape our loneliness. Thus, seeking to satisfy our curiosity can lead to situations that satisfy so many of our other, deeper longings. The rewards for seeking to establish new relationships can be enormous.

The Rewards of Curiosity

To reap these rewards, of course, we must fall back onto the reverence that curiosity entails. We must treat others, especially those very different from us, with respect as we ask them to divulge to us their hearts and histories. Without this, we run the risk of being exploitative or insensitive. Without the right kind of sensitivity in these situations, the process short circuits, leading to closure on the part of at least one party and the end of information exchange that might satiate burning curiosity.

Just as the rewards for initiating new relationships can be significant, so can the risks. Relationships entail greater risk than solo endeavors because we cannot simply change the channel on someone we don't like. Even to get a new relationship off the ground, we must surrender some measure of control, and so are less able to isolate ourselves from the consequences of poor choices.

We may cause hurt feelings. We may have our feelings hurt. We may behave in ways that cause enduring embarrassment to ourselves or others. Any of these is possible, of course. But none are a reason to avoid allowing our curiosity to drive us toward others. As with all valuable enterprises, the risk simply must be accepted. As we practice establishing new relationships, our skills will develop and, in time, we will not need to worry so much about the negative possibilities of following where our desire to know has led us.

Finally, we can allow our curiosity to lead us into experiencing new ideas. At first blush, this might seem like the hardest area for us to experience new things. Some of us don't read much, don't spend our spare time watching lectures on YouTube. How then can we experience new ideas? There are a couple of ways.

First, new ideas can come from within our own minds. If we allow them to, our minds can easily fall into a rut. Our thoughts become repetitive and unproductive, but a little effort can make our thinking more fertile. We can pay attention to the content of our thoughts. This has two advantages. When we become more aware of what we are thinking, we become more capable of simply choosing not to allow our reflexive, repetitive thoughts to run rampant. We can make space for inner silence. We can quiet our anxious thoughts. This will allow new ideas, new possibilities we had not previously considered to come through.

New ideas can also come to us through other people. To access ideas in this way, we must learn to listen. If we approach people with a resolute unwillingness to at least hear their thoughts before we begin insisting on our own, we miss the opportunity to experience the doors in us that their unique insights might open.

When we encounter new ideas, growth happens. Ultimately, we may not believe these new ideas are right or true. But, if we are willing to consider them in light of our previous emotional and intellectual commitments, growth will happen. Through encountering these ideas and forming new responses to them we become a fuller person. Even if the encounter with a new idea means we become better able to articulate why we reject it, we are still fuller and better than we were before discovering it.

Conversely, we may decide that we can accept the new idea. Perhaps this new idea we have stumbled upon fits well with our prior intellectual and emotional commitments. If this is the case, we cannot help but grow. This idea may be a missing piece to a puzzle, filling a hole in our understanding, making that understanding more whole. Allowing our curiosity to drive us toward new ideas leads us to see our lives and the world in new ways. The incurious person's worldview is locked and frozen; the worldview of the curious is always being refined, becoming more detailed and comprehensive daily.

Just as there were risks involved with allowing our curiosity to drive us toward new experiences and relationships, engaging with new ideas also involves risks. Because ideas are abstract, meaning they only exist in the mind, it might be easy to think that the risks they present are less serious than those presented by either new experiences or new relationships.

Nothing could be further from the truth. Ideas are the foundation of all our interpretations of events and of our behavior. Allowing ideas to influence us involves risk at a much more fundamental level. If we were to accept enough bad ideas, we would grow unhappy, our behavior would become either unproductive or destructive.

For this reason, making sure that even while we are open to encountering new ideas, we remain rooted in previously adopted truths is critical. Fortunately, it is not as if we have no clue what kind of ideas lead to what kind of results. We know from the long human history of reflecting on these matters that some ideas produce better fruit than others.

If we are rooted in a tradition of wisdom, we need not fear encountering any idea because we have some means of judging its value. Ideas that complement the wisdom we have already accrued should be accepted, those contrary to it, should be rejected. With this kind of confidence, no one need fear new ideas. In fact, having internalized this bedrock wisdom sets us free to explore the intellectual world fully while always being able to find our way home.

Since it is clear now that curiosity is a good thing, we must ask whether it is possible to awaken curiosity when it has gone dormant. Can a person whose growth has stagnated suddenly cause himself to desire growth?

Yes and no.

The no part of the answer stems from the fact that arrogance, irreverence and provincialism all work against the possibility of stimulating new growth in oneself. People deeply scripted in these traits tend to be unconscious of them. The arrogant do not think of themselves as arrogant, the irreverent do not see themselves as lacking reverence. Those people are unlikely to make a change toward becoming more curious.

But the news is not all bad. The good news is that sensing a need to branch out, desiring new growth is evidence of not being totally lost within the maze of these negative traits. The better news is that even those with but a spark of curiosity in them can fan that spark into a roaring flame that fuels productive growth.

Developing Curiosity

People with enough awareness to want to increase their level of curiosity can do so. But first, they must realize that curiosity doesn't grow just by doing things that satisfy it. It doesn't grow by simply doing new things alone. Its growth also requires conscious commitment. People who realize they desire to know more, to be and to do more, and who commit to that goal are more likely to achieve it.

Step one is to make a conscious commitment. This means recognizing and accepting that limits to your knowledge exist and being willing to find them. Begin doing whatever is required to make your boundaries less restrictive by following your natural curiosity. But what if you have very little natural curiosity? That too can be encouraged. You can increase your level of curiosity in several ways.

Make a list of things you are interested in, or of things that resonate with or speak to you. Make a list of places, people and things that make you feel happy and positive. Then, beneath each one, make a list of questions about them. These might include, "Where did he/ she/ they/ it come from?" "What do I like about this?" Or "How do they do it?" In general, you can always ask about history. You can always ask about meaning.

Once you have a list of questions, start seeking answers. This process might involve looking at books, doing searches on the Internet, or talking to experts. Do whatever is necessary to fill the gaps in your knowledge about the things you love. As you do this, here is what you will find: more questions. Find the answer to those. Repeat the process.

As you do this, your curiosity will grow. You will have to trust yourself, trust that by following your natural desire to know, you will be guiding yourself down a path toward greater fulfillment, toward actualizing the person you could be. Even when things get scary or the risks mount, you will have to trust yourself to carry on.

But don't worry. As you engage this process, you will cease having to push so hard as the forces of life will engage and begin pulling you forward as new opportunities to learn and serve open up for you. At that point, you will be moving forward powered only in part by curiosity. The love and reverence for life that underlies your desire to know will have increased and become a source of power.

And that is why curiosity is important to cultivate. Because without it, we cannot treat life fully as a gift. Only by being open, curious and brave can we truly be receptive to the wonders that lie in this world and beyond. When we are otherwise—incurious, arrogant, hard and small—we do not appreciate. We cannot take joy. Through consistently, consciously cultivating our curiosity we will know and not in our minds alone, but in our hearts as well, more than we once could have imagined.

18

Non-Attachment

The Roller Coaster of Attachment

A COUPLE OF YEARS ago, I stopped watching the news. I realized that the news, as C. John Somerville has pointed out, was making us dumb[1]. It makes us dumb not in the sense that we lose IQ points by watching it (though anecdotal evidence suggests this is true), but because it creates in us a false impression of what the world is like. Through consuming a steady diet of the news, we are conditioned to focus our attention on daily shifts in power and random events occurring around the world. We become addicted to the product of the news industry which Sommerville rightly says is "change."

When we become a spectator, the whole world becomes a show. We watch entranced as the daily dramas of power unfold. We tune in to see what happens next in the world, but we stay because of what is happening inside us. We become attached to players in the drama. We get invested in outcomes. Our inner lives get caught up in the workings of the world we see on the screen. We become so attached to the change we are being sold that we lose our connection to what is permanent.

We begin to experience inwardly the upheaval we witness in the outside world. As the daily roller coaster goes up, we feel ourselves inwardly lifted. Our side is winning! When the coaster descends, we go down with it. Our side is losing! Our new discouragement does not, however, keep us from watching the news. It does the opposite. Now that we know that things are very, very bad and that our side is losing, we must tune in to the

---

1. Sommerville John *How the News Makes Us Dumb*.

next broadcast or check out the newest social media posts to try to recover. We stay tuned, hoping the tides will shift.

They always do. Sooner or later, the crisis of the moment passes and we take a deep breath. Then we enter a lull in which we review the crises just passed or prognosticate about what the next crisis will be. Eventually, another crisis hits, and we begin the process again.

The news is just one of the areas of life where we experience this kind of roller coaster. If we look closely, we can see that many other areas of life operate in similar ways. Take fashion, for example. A person who follows fashions and hopes to be seen as au Courant, will find that her moods follow her hemlines. As styles go in and out of popularity, her sense of pride and stability will rise and fall according to how current her wardrobe appears.

American high school is a similar roller coaster, replete as it is with its own vicious politics. The days when we feel our social stock rising, we're up. When one of the cool kids snubs us, we're down. Our position in the social hierarchy is, we feel, precarious, and so we must remain on guard lest something upends it.

We can feel the same about our financial lives. We mirror the market. It's up, we're up. It's down, we're down. We monitor our accounts. When one gets larger, we cheer. When one shrinks, we fear. We cycle through this process payday after payday for most of our lives.

Beyond all these, we tend to suffer this kind of up and down existence in our personal lives. In families and other relationships, our inner peace tends to rest on the shaky foundation of our perceptions of others' attitudes, beliefs and behaviors. If they are well-disposed toward us, then we are happy. If they are rude or unfair, we are disturbed. We may go to great lengths trying to change their beliefs, values and behaviors in order to restore our own equilibrium.

On the other hand, we may strategically disapprove of others to get them to do whatever is necessary to please us. When they do, we have a sense of power and feel that we can relax. When they will not do our bidding, our anxiety and rage increase. We become far too invested in the choices of others, as if we believed our very lives depend on others' doing what we want, on things going our way, on our side winning.

Getting Off the Ride

In short, we are thoroughly attached to the outcomes of various circumstances in the world, and so long as we are attached, we will never live a life of peace. To break free and grow toward our full maturity, we must cultivate non-attachment. We must unhook our inner lives from the shifting circumstances around us and hook them to what is stable, immutable and permanent.

Before we begin examining what non-attachment means, let's lay out some things it does not mean. Non-attachment does not mean coldness. It does not mean that we cease to care about the welfare of others. It does not mean we cultivate an attitude of indifference or apathy. Living in non-attachment does not mean pretending we do not live in a world where the consequences of our choices affect us. Non-attachment does not mean that we have no emotional connection to others or to the meaning of events.

People who pretend otherwise may have an appearance of non-attachment, but it is an appearance only. In fact, the attitudes listed above, ranging from apathy to anger to pretending, are all examples of what happens when we remain deeply attached to the ups and downs of the world and become disappointed. Far from being examples of non-attachment, these destructive approaches are examples of attachment taken to its deadliest extreme.

So then, what is non-attachment?

Outcome Independence Is the Key

The chief component of non-attachment is outcome independence. To break free of our attachments to the volatile circumstances of life. We must learn to be independent of the possible outcomes we might face.

What does outcome independence look like?

In life, we repeatedly find ourselves in situations where the outcome is uncertain. Will I get into that school I applied to? Will I get the job I wanted? Will she say yes? Life is often hard to predict. There is much we cannot know, and yet, often we must act, and act without full and exhaustive knowledge.

Our natural tendency is to be anxious about the outcomes of all these situations, to worry about what will happen. Often, we go so far as to try to control the people and decisions involved. All because we have become so hooked into the rising and falling action of life that we believe our well-being is dependent on a specific outcome. This pattern yields a terrifying and fruitless way to live.

Outcome independence means we are not consumed with worry about what will happen. Rather, while we might desire a specific outcome, even ardently so, we are relaxed and trusting. We know that if this opportunity doesn't materialize, we'll be fine. People who are outcome independent think in terms of abundance. They know that there is always another school to apply to, another job to interview for, another girl to ask out.

Outcome independence itself can be broken down into a few component parts. One is confidence. The higher our confidence in our abilities to handle adversity, to weather the storms of life, the less we will be caught up in thinking any individual situation MUST have a specific outcome. If we face some undesirable outcomes, we will know we are able to handle them. Problems, we tell ourselves, difficult though they may be, are not impossible to solve.

This kind of confidence has multiple sources. Some of it may come from having grown up in environments we found safe and edifying. In such environments we may have been encouraged to face challenges and told we were adequate to meet them. We may have been taught skills, had good role models. All these things help develop our confidence. When someone we esteem believes that what we are is sufficient to meet the problems of life, believing this about ourselves becomes easier. When we are introduced to the problems of life by someone able to protect and instruct us, we will feel more confident facing those problems when we must do so alone.

Having grown up in a nurturing environment, however, is not a necessity for confidence. Coming from such an environment helps, but lacking it does not doom anyone to a life with no confidence. This is because, ultimately, confidence comes from solving problems, and anyone can improve his problem-solving skills at any point in life.

And as we improve our problem-solving skills, our confidence improves. The result of a long string of solved problems is the conviction that we will be able to solve the next one that comes along. A deep sense that we can handle the problems we encounter reduces our anxiety and therefore makes us less dependent on any situation's outcome. The less dependent we are on the outcome of a situation, the less attached we are.

A second component of outcome independence is an abundance mentality. Stephen Covey defines an abundance mentality as "the paradigm that there is plenty out there for everybody".[2] People with this paradigm see the world as able to meet not only their needs but also those of all the others inhabiting it. An abundance mindset is a component of outcome independence, because it means knowing that even if any particular situation results in a bad outcome, more opportunities will arise. We do not live under the illusion that our lives and futures are entirely dependent on what happens in this one situation. If the school we wanted to go to rejects us, we know we will go to school elsewhere. We know that if we get turned down for a job, other opportunities will present themselves. We know that if we don't get a date with with one we had our eye on, there are plenty of others who will accept our invitations.

Having an abundance mentality does not mean pretending. Going on a spending spree when you've only got eleven dollars in the bank is not an abundance mentality. Having an abundance mentality does not mean pretending there is more of anything than there is. It means not allowing fear and anxiety to narrow your field of vision so greatly that you fail to see the abundance that is clearly all around us. Rather than being a means of make-believe, an abundance mentality is a way of connecting to the reality that there is more available to us than we will ever consume. Seeing this reality ups our confidence.

Two things that make the idea of abundance easier to accept are having an ultimate goal in our minds and believing in a larger plan. Without an overall goal for what we want to achieve in life, we will easily fall into believing that any of the stepping stones we use to get to it are, in fact, the ultimate goal.

Let's return to the example of getting into a specific, perhaps prestigious, school. This is the kind of thing many young people become obsessed with, and for good reason. The standard cultural narrative for a long time has been that getting into the "best" schools leads to the "best" lives. This view, however, is myopic.

One reason we grow so attached to specific outcomes is that we believe that if a specific outcome is not achieved, we are sunk. If we believe the end goal is to attend a particular university, and then are denied that opportunity, our inner peace will quickly be destroyed. However, if our ultimate goal is something like "to do as much good for others as possible," we can see that there are many paths to achieving that goal. Any particular situation, regardless of its outcome, is unlikely to derail us from our ultimate

---

2. Covey Stephen *The Seven Habits of Highly Effective People*, 219.

goal. With this kind of ultimate goal in mind, we can see that there are many schools we could attend which would do a good job preparing us to do good for others no matter which professional field of endeavor we wish to pursue. This too increases the confidence with which we approach life.

When we see that there are many paths to achieving our goals, we no longer need to attach to a specific means of getting there. We are more confident about moving forward, knowing that if one path is blocked, we will simply find another way. Our faith that we will one day achieve this goal need not be shaken merely because the means we had anticipated using have proven unworkable. By being clear about our ultimate goal we can deal with unforeseen set-backs with aplomb.

Believing in a larger plan helps too. Most commonly this means belief in God's will, but one does not have to believe in God to believe that the events of our lives are unfolding in accord with a higher plan. To believe this does not mean believing that individual choices don't matter, but only that when we encounter unforeseen difficulties or when we are disappointed by the outcome of events, we need not despair because we have a sense that developments are being directed in harmony with some plan we cannot see. If we believe this plan is benevolent, we can more easily assume an attitude of non-attachment toward the situations we face.

We can become calloused to the idea that reality is unfolding according to a plan because we so often hear this sentiment expressed in cliches. "Everything happens for a reason" is an example. Believing that everything happens for a reason is an easy way to comfort ourselves over minor losses. It might make us feel better when we can't find a good parking spot and end up a few minutes late for an appointment. It might not work so well when we confront the death of a child or some other truly terrible suffering.

Exploring this idea in detail would require a book of its own. In fact, many books have been written exploring this topic. The point to make here is simply that holding a belief that reality is directed by some force to some end makes cultivating non-attachment easier. When we have a sense of being moved or directed toward a good end by some power beyond ourselves, we don't need to struggle as hard to control or to engineer outcomes Holding this kind of belief, however, is not necessary for having an attitude of non-attachment. Though non-attachment can be cultivated without this belief, asking ourselves what we believe about this issue is critical work we are all beholden to do.

Non-Attachment

Neglecting this work is a large part of why we end up so attached to particular outcomes in the first place. And not just outcomes either. We can be attached to all sorts of things.

One term we often use for these kinds of attachments is addiction. Certainly some addictions have physiological components, but they all also have a component of mental and psychological attachment. If they did not, if we were not psychologically attached to some physical object or behavior, we would not be addicted. Because substance addictions, whether to alcohol or other drugs, have such a pronounced physical component, it's easier to see the role of emotional and psychological attachment when we consider behavioral addictions.

Imagine a young man in his late 20's who is single, lives alone and works a job he doesn't particularly like. Let's call him Jared. Think about his day and the many things and behaviors on which he depends to allow him to function. When he wakes up in the morning, he is focused on getting the coffee he needs to help him wake up. He depends on the radio or a funny podcast to keep him entertained and distracted during a painful commute. At work, he furtively surfs the Internet or scrolls social media on his phone to ease the pain of his boring and restrictive work. Late in the afternoon, he hits the vending machine for an afternoon fix of chips and soft drink to keep him going. On the way home, another podcast. Once he is at home, he spends his evenings playing video games or watching television to help him cope with the dread of going back to work the next day.

Now do not think that I am saying all of this is bad. Of course, we all depend on many external pleasures to help us cope with the pressures and demands of life. The point is that many of us engage in these kinds of behaviors even when doing so has demonstrably negative consequences. The fact that Jared has a cup of coffee in the morning doesn't mean that Jared has a problem. If, however, one cup grows to 15 throughout the day, Jared has a problem.

Largely, these behaviors and the attachments behind them become problems because they are unconscious. We become attached to these things because we do not admit to ourselves that we are using them to cope. When we are unconscious of our reasons for why we do what we do, we are vulnerable to falling into excessive use. One cup of coffee made us feel better when we were low, a part of us reasons, so another will make us feel even better. We repeat this pattern again and again until the attachment is difficult to break.

Our attachments to the outcomes of life situations motivate our dependence on external substances and behaviors. When we grow anxious about the outcome of a situation, we are tempted to change our feelings through the use of an external substance or negative behavior. Thus do we fall into cycles of greater dependency and attachment.

Reversing this pattern requires cultivating non-attachment. If we can get free from the need to control the outcomes of our situations, we will feel more peace. More peace allows us to become more conscious and in control of our decisions about how and when and to what degree we indulge behaviors which, while they might provide short term relief, have long-term negative consequences. When we cultivate non-attachment, we become freer and, when we become freer, more of our authentic selves can emerge.

Moving toward Non-Attachment

What to do then to begin moving toward non-attachment if we are deeply stuck in the attachments we formed long ago and are being made miserable by them?

The first step is to recognize that we are attached. For many of us, living with attachments to outcomes or to external objects and behaviors is second nature. We have never asked whether there might be a way to live that doesn't require us to be on an emotional roller coaster every day of our lives. We assume external events cause our inner reactions. Many of us never consider whether we have a choice in these matters at all.

Well, we do. We can choose how attached to be to things and we can decide what, if anything, to be attached to. We can choose to attach to virtue, wisdom, and the permanent unchanging principles that govern human affairs.

But we can do none of this if we remain unconscious about our attachments. So, begin observing and noticing without judgement how frequently you feel invested in making sure a situation has a particular outcome, and how frequently you find yourself turning to a substance or behavior hoping it will change your feelings.

As you do this, you will notice that your attachments are many. Some will be stronger than others. Break the weaker ones first. Maybe you are in a situation where the repair shop is unsure if your car will be ready in two days or in three. You might notice that you have some concern about this even though your transportation needs are met in other

Non-Attachment

ways. Tell yourself that you are ok, that you will get where you need to go. Consciously work to alter your attitude to the point where you are at peace with either possible outcome.

Some outcomes will be harder to detach from. Maybe you are especially concerned about one of your children going to college. If you are attached to his going, you may attempt to influence him. You may try the aggressive route, hectoring and threatening big consequences if he doesn't go. Maybe you'll choose the more subtle route of dropping hints and brochures around the house. Either way, your attempts to engineer an outcome are likely to backfire, thus creating the outcome you most fear. When your attachment to a specific outcome is especially strong, you must work even harder to break it. In these situations, it is necessary to understand that people are free to make their own choices, even when they might choose in a way we would not like them to. Remind yourself that whatever others choose, you are free to make the choices that are best for you and that through exercising your power to choose, you will remain safe and secure regardless of the choices of others.

Accepting that you simply do not have the power to control anything other than your choices is central to making this shift. Many of our attachments are, in fact, born out of our illusions of control. We tend to imagine that we can or, at least, should be able to control more. Surrendering that illusion and accepting the limits of our power is the cornerstone of non-attachment. When you feel your concern growing over a situation, bring your attention back to the question, "Is there anything I can do about this?" If the answer is yes, do that thing and then relax. If the answer is no, just relax.

You will notice as you ask yourself this question, that one thing that won't help is to turn to your favorite substance or behavioral attachments. Focusing on the question "Is there anything I can do about this?" orients you toward positive action. Do this enough and you will see how turning to your preferred mood-altering habits is not positive action.

As you train yourself to take positive action where it is possible and to surrender where it is not, you will find that you need your external mood-altering attachments less. Taking action and then relaxing both alter your mood. When you begin to draw limits for yourself about what you will and will not be concerned about, it becomes easier to draw limits for yourself about what you will and will not do.

The result of cultivating non-attachment is not passivity but greater initiative and action because we accept that our actions are all we can control. When we recognize that while we cannot control outcomes, we can influence them through our actions non-attachment leads not to less love for and commitment to our lives, but infinitely more.

As we weaken our attachments to the shifting circumstances in the world, we will find ourselves functioning with a new level of consciousness. We will see how the principles we apply to our decisions routinely guide us toward growth and peace. We will come to love not only our lives, but the wisdom that guides them. When we arrive at this place, we know that our attachments lie no longer with the vicissitudes of daily life, but with the truths that anchor us amidst them. Just as a ship has but one attachment to its anchor, and yet remains steady, we will find that a single attachment to the permanent things suffices to keep us moored.

19

Love

Love and Virtue

IN SPITE OF WHAT we have all been told by a million pop songs and made for tv movies, love is more than emotion. Love is more than mere a flutter in the stomach or an extra rush of the blood. Love is a virtue, and in fact, it is the ground of all the others.

Given our conditioning, it might sound strange to write about love as a virtue we can cultivate. Many modern people are wholeheartedly devoted to the notion of love as a mere feeling, a surge of emotion in the presence of another. How could something like that, something spontaneous and free-flowing, be a virtue we can cultivate?

It can't. Fortunately, when modern people think this is what love is, modern people are wrong. That rush of emotion is something called limerence, a passing psychological state that involves attraction to another and the desire to form a more intimate relationship. Limerence is involuntary. We choose to show love. Only qualities we can choose to exhibit can be virtues. Limerence therefore is not a virtue because we cannot choose it over the long course of a lifetime. We cannot make a habit of transient limerence.

The receiving of love is not a virtue either. Virtue is the habit of choosing the Good. The other virtues we have examined in this book are all components of or pieces of what the Good entails. Because we cannot choose to have other people give us love, being loved cannot itself be a virtue. Whether people love us is not something our choices control.

Love is unique. It is not technically merely a component of the Good as other virtues are. Love is different. Love is a virtue because we can choose to cultivate it in ourselves, but it is also the grounding of the virtuous life. Love motivates virtue. Love is the reason we want to choose the Good in the first place.

Our Fundamental Posture

When we want to cultivate the virtue of love in ourselves, what, exactly, are we cultivating? At its base, we are cultivating an attitude toward others and toward life itself. In the chapter on resentment, I said many people resent reality. Love is the opposite path. Love approaches reality with gratitude, humbly accepting what is as a gift.

This attitude leads to a fundamental goodwill toward reality and all it entails. Rather than being resentful, the loving person embraces what is presented to him, seeing it as beautiful, valuable and temporary. The loving person is always a little in awe of what is real. Tom Junod in an article for Esquire magazine about Fred Rogers, wrote, "Mr. Rogers lives in a state astonishment."[1] This sentence is a good description of the person whose fundamental orientation toward life is loving.

Just as the behavior and beliefs of the resentful person stem from his bedrock apprehension of life as unfair, so the beliefs and behaviors of the loving person spring from his underlying posture toward life. When his basic response to reality is love, resentment and other vices may be present at times, but they will not root themselves deeply and thus will die away with time.

Because the loving person's fundamental orientation toward life and reality is one of awe and appreciation, she seeks to preserve and to enhance the people and situations she encounters. Her basic appreciation of life manifests in her choices. She looks for ways to serve others and to make them stronger.

This does not mean love is easy for her. It does mean that she never sees virtue as an imposition. To her virtue is not a heavy burden, but rather a vehicle through which she can express her joy and awe about the mere fact of existence. In short, at least most of the time, she wants to be virtuous, and virtue is easier to cultivate for those who actually want to do so.

---

1. Junod, http://www.neighborhoodarchive.com/publications/press/esquire/index.html.

All this together: the fundamental gratitude for existence, the desire to respond to the gift of life through service, to encourage the growth of others, to choose the Good, these together we call love.

Love as Power

Love is, above all, power. It is from love that we derive the power to choose the good consistently. Love creates in us the desire to respond to the gift of life by giving good gifts in return. Love generates the energy necessary to overcome all the forces that would interfere with our life of gift giving which is the life of virtue.

The life of virtue is impossible without this sort of power. In life we encounter the force mentioned earlier, that force Stephen Pressfield calls simply "resistance."[2] Resistance is the part of reality that pushes back. Resistance resists. When we set our minds to changing some bad habit or to cultivating some new good habit, resistance resists. When we try to improve a relationship, resistance resists. Resistance pushes back on all our noble intentions and fancy aspirations. It seeks to undermine our courage and invites us as seductively as possible to give up.

We all know this from experience. As soon as we take the first modest step in some positive new direction, we find ourselves met by an obstacle, some sort of pushback. Resistance is what makes accomplishing anything good an admirable feat. We admire people who achieve things because we know that achieving anything requires overcoming resistance.

Resistance can come in many ways and at varying levels of intensity. Let's say you decide to begin walking every day first thing in the morning. You imagine yourself strolling outdoors. In your mind, you see yourself enjoying the sunshine and the fresh air. Birds are singing and the flowers are in bloom. You can feel your stress melting away. You imagine how much trimmer and healthier this habit will make you. You get excited, determined to begin the next morning.

The next morning, it rains. At the moment, you are encountering resistance, and you must make a choice about how you will respond. You have three options. You can push on, you can give up or you can resolve to try again later. Option three might seem attractive, but when you try later, resistance will be there too. You can only choose option three so many times before you must choose either option one or option two.

2. Pressfield, *The War of Art*, 4

Most people choose option two. Most people give up. They don't do it consciously. They don't say to themselves, "My commitment to walking was just a sham. I don't want to begin walking everyday unless it is always going to be convenient and can be done under the most agreeable circumstances possible." No, they just shrug and say to themselves, "maybe tomorrow." Eventually, they option three themselves right into option two. Giving up but disguising it as postponement is a lot easier than admitting we are giving up at the first sign of resistance.

Developing a life of virtue demands we choose option one more often than not. Just as with physical goals, we will meet resistance when we begin making efforts to improve our level of virtue. Any resolution to practice self-discipline will be immediately met by resistance, either in the form of freshly baked cookies, an unusually comfortable bed, or an ill-tempered coworker.

To develop a new level of virtue, we must have power. That power is love. When we connect to love for ourselves, for others, and for the world—we will find that we are more able to make the difficult choice to exercise option one, to carry through with the actions we know will elevate us by enhancing our character.

Love empowers us in at least two ways. First, it adds meaning to our choices, and, second, it rewards us with positive emotions. One way we overcome resistance in the pursuit of virtue is by seeing clearly how new levels of virtue will benefit those around us, those who are important to us.

The pursuit of virtue, even our own virtue, is never ours alone. Rather, we pursue it for our own sake and for the sakes of others. When we become more patient, more curious, more disciplined, we make the lives of those around us better. We become more pleasant to be around. Everyone knows this instinctively. No one has ever thought to himself, "This person I am with is too considerate, too generous and too self-controlled, I want to go spend my time with someone more self-centered, frivolous and indulgent." We all want to be around people with more virtue rather than less.

Since this is true for each of us, we can easily reason that it is true for all others we encounter. Since we know others prefer to be with people who are virtuous and pleasant, we can know that by making ourselves more virtuous and pleasant we are giving a gift to those around us. We make ourselves someone more enjoyable to be around by making ourselves someone with greater virtue. But we do not just make ourselves more pleasant, we actually increase our capacity for relationships.

The way of virtue is to choose option one. The way of virtue means not shirking from the resolutions we have made when we encounter resistance, if not for our own sakes, then in order to create a more pleasant and rewarding life for those we spend most of our time around. Thus does love motivate us to overcome.

Love also expands our positive emotions and experiences as we repeatedly choose option one. If on that morning when it is raining, we choose not to go for a walk, we will know we have broken a promise to ourselves. Consistently breaking promises to ourselves takes an emotional toll. In spite of our justifications, we grow more and more discouraged as the broken promises pile up.

The emotional impact of this can be felt in multiple ways. We may feel out of control. Because being out of control is frightening, our anxiety will go up. We might also feel depressed, or at least have a dull feeling of being less and less engaged in the world and less and less interested in our own futures. Because we know in our depths that keeping promises to oneself is the slow, steady way to a better future, when we fail to keep them, we find our vision of the future growing dimmer and more gray and our passion for it reduced.

Keeping promises to ourselves is an act of love. When we love ourselves in this way, we eventually begin to see ourselves differently. Through expressing our self-love in the form of kept promises, we develop greater self-respect, and self-respect feels good. The internal sense of good feelings grows the more we practice. At some point, we begin to notice that we are more optimistic about our futures, the world appears less dark to us. These good feelings about ourselves are part of the rewards of employing the power of love to grow.

But our emotional changes need not be confined merely to how we feel about ourselves. The way we feel about the world at large is also likely to change. This does not mean we will cease to see what is painful or tragic in the world, nor does not mean that we begin pretending those things are not as awful as they are. But, just as love leads to virtue, pursuing virtue leads to a more loving disposition toward life.

As we pursue the virtues love empowers, we begin to focus more exclusively on what is within our power. We find that we are able to respond to the tragic nature of the world not with fear or a sense of being overwhelmed, but with greater energy for doing what we can to mitigate negative realities.

We cease to see ourselves exclusively as beings affected by what happens and start to see ourselves as beings capable of making things happen.

The more our focus moves from what Stephen Covey called our circle of concern, which contains all the things we might be worried about, to our circles of control and influence, which contain all the things over which we have some degree of power, the more we feel better about ourselves and the world[3]. As we see ourselves making a positive impact in tangible ways, the world becomes less scary and capricious and instead becomes the field in which we encounter opportunity after opportunity to do good.

Virtue rooted in love also helps us radiate good feelings to others. When we are truly grateful for the gift of life, when we are at peace inwardly, it shows. Many people are naturally drawn to others who radiate this kind of peace and gratitude.

As others are drawn toward us, they bring with them all sorts of rewards. When others trust us because of the virtues evident in us, virtues built on our fundamentally loving response to existence, they want to work with us. As we work together with others, our potential to do good multiplies. When we join with others, our capacity to create positive change intensifies beyond what a single individual can do or imagine. This is the reward of love: membership in a community devoted to doing good in creative and unforeseen ways.

Actualizing this community depends on our habits. Virtuous habits conquer resistance, or at least, reduce it to a more manageable level. Love, because it empowers virtue, is the engine of good habits.

Most of us focus on the habits of virtue that we have the hardest time mastering. Sometimes we do this to the point of believing we have no real habits of virtue. This is untrue. Most of us have virtuous habits we don't even think about, habits which take no effort whatsoever to live out. Most of us routinely go into stores and never even think about stealing any of the items on display. For most of us, our habit of not shoplifting is so engrained we are not even conscious of it. The goal of growing in virtue is to choose what I called option one above over and over again until it becomes a habit as unconscious as our habit of not committing petty theft.

We rarely get to this point because change is hard, and the hardest part of any change is the beginning. Our old ways exert a gravitational force that pulls us downward. We give up because we do not have the power necessary to overcome resistance long enough to establish a reflexive habit.

---

3. Covey, *The Seven Habits of Highly Effective People*, 81

Think of it this way: for a rocket to get into space, it must have power, must have sufficient fuel to push through the resistance of earth's gravitational pull. Once in space much less fuel is required. So it is with us; the greatest power requirements are at the launch of any new virtuous habit.

Why then is it so hard to establish these new habits? The simple answer is that we do not have enough fuel, enough love. I am not saying we are incapable of love. That is not the case. All of us had enough fuel to reach whatever heights we have reached. A mother who knows she is too involved in social media and ought to put her phone down and pay more attention to her child is not devoid of love for him; she is merely trapped in an orbit she does not have enough energy to escape.

To break through the atmosphere of her own habits and history, she is going to require more fuel, more love. This means that there will have to be input before there is output. No one can burn fuel she does not have. No one can rely on the power of a love that is not present.

So, when faced with both a habit she cannot break and an urgent desire to do so, this mother must find a means of connecting to the power of love. Fortunately, there are lots of ways of doing that. Many of us have a sense of how to do this already. We already have a sense of what things empower, cheer and fulfill us. The problem isn't that we don't recognize these things, the problem is that we neglect them.

Cultivating Love

How then should this mother overcome her cell phone fixation? The answer requires another word about discipline. Discipline is helpful in maintaining good habits. The desire to control oneself and to do what growth requires is good and right, but neither desire nor a teeth-gritting determination alone will actually power through resistance long enough to land us in a new orbit. To do that, we must have an additional infusion of fuel.

Because the fuel for growth in virtue is love, there must be a way for it to flow both in and out. Both paths must be clear and open if we are to achieve our goal. Let's talk first about what it means to have love flow in. Flowing in requires some source of love external to us. If we want to move to a new level in our growth, we must connect to some entity able to fill us.

Many people meet this need in faith. God, who is the inexhaustible source of love, fuels us. If we cannot connect to some conception of God or to other spiritual resources, we can at least turn to reality in all its wonder.

Connecting with realities that inspire wonder is critical. The chief way to do this is through contemplation. Contemplation is a mental activity certainly, but not like the kind of analytical thinking we engage in when we problem solve. Rather, contemplation is a kind of mental beholding. It increases our awareness of the loveliness and strangeness of existence without analysis. Contemplation puts us in touch with a gratitude that moves us toward the ultimate yes to life in spite of everything. The stronger our yes, the more power we will find flowing into us.

People who can say only a weak yes to life must reflect on why. There are many reasons why this may be the case. The most common is unresolved hurts and trauma which still control us. The more we seek to engage life from behind our defenses, the weaker our yes will be. The weaker our yes, the lower our power.

The greatest act of love a person can extend to himself is to confront his early traumas, to change the patterns of thought and feeling they established within him. This allows him to lower his defenses. When defenses are lowered, the wonder and strangeness of existence can more easily flow in. The more they flow in, the stronger his yes can grow.

Saying yes to life is not enough. We must be connected to others through a bond of love. We cannot reach new levels of growth and virtue alone. People seeking to take on more love must be intentional about cultivating relationships that encourage it. In one sense, all relationships do this. If we have an appropriate sense of awe and wonder regarding those we encounter, even casual meetings can offer us a bit of what we need.

Casual relationships alone, however, will not suffice. We require others operating at levels similar to our own. We need people who share our values, interests and outlook in order to really create the kind of connection that fuels us. We require friends.

These can be hard to find in today's frenetic culture which has stupefied so many into a consumerist haze. Fortunately, it has never been easier to connect with others who live far from you. Online communities give us the chance to find the kind of connections we need in ways unencumbered by physical space. While it may be true that nothing exceeds the impact of face-to-face interactions, it is also true that few of us have the luxury of having a group of the exact sort of individuals we need living nearby.

Once we have established the sources of love that fill us, we are ready to burn some fuel. We are ready to let the love flow out from us. Here is where discipline becomes important. When we have the proper fuel in the

Love

form of love from self and others, we are ready to once again try launching ourselves to a new level.

With the proper flow of fuel, our chances of success are greatly enhanced. When we have the proper fuel, we can overcome resistance that tries to hold us back. When we have settled into a new altitude, we will find that our opportunities to fuel others are greater. The higher your altitude, the more chances to pull others up you will have. And this is the ultimate reason to pursue a life of love, because it allows us to elevate not just ourselves but others in a way that offers us the chance to see them take off for heights previously unknown.

20

Virtue and Happiness

The Reasons for Our Unhappiness

WHAT IS THE POINT of all this exploration? Is there some end toward which all this effort to cultivate virtue and overcome vice is directed? What is the goal of all this work?

At the beginning of this book, I wrote that virtues are those character traits which encourage human growth. I said that we hold within ourselves a natural plan of development that we are inclined to follow. Virtues help us to follow that plan. I also said that the state of flourishing in which we move toward our ideal selves is happiness.

Since this is true, since we all have within us a map and a plan for our growth and flourishing, why is it that so many people are unhappy?

Three reasons will suffice. First, we have been taught to separate our character, our habits of choosing the Good, from our subjective feeling of happiness. Second, we naturally externalize our quest for happiness, and third, we are encouraged to pursue distraction rather than happiness.

We have all long been taught that happiness is unpredictable, a random fleeting state that settles on us once in a while for no discernible reason. We are not taught that a sense of fulfillment and excitement that we might call happiness is connected in any way to our choices, to our character.

In popular culture, people who emphasize character and personal responsibility are portrayed as anything but happy. In our culture's dominant narrative, concern about character and responsibility are the domain of the dour. Only pinch-faced, bitter scorekeepers are concerned with such matters, we are told. We are led to believe people concerned with these things are driven by a quest for power, and a desire to make others feel inferior in order to to mask their own inner demons.

As with most ideas pushed by our popular culture, this one is false. Contrary to what we are routinely taught, character is not an impediment to happiness. Character is the capacity for happiness. By growing in virtue, we expand the amount of joy and gratitude we can hold. We increase our ability to manage and avoid problems. We create better circumstances for ourselves and others. This, and not indulgence, is what happiness is.

So, it stands to reason that if we desire to increase our happiness, we must increase our virtue. This should not, at this point, be hard to see. We can easily see how a life of vice, a life that is self-centered, frivolous, undignified and indulgent leads, in the end, to misery. We can easily see too that a life that is balanced, ordered, serious and connected leads to greater peace and satisfaction.

The annals of history are filled with stories of people who believed that impulsivity, hedonism and indulgence would bring lasting joy only to find that idea was false. Many of us have walked this path ourselves. Even if this only means we realized that third piece of pie was making us feel worse not better, we have had enough experience to know that our level of happiness is related to our moral choices.

This all becomes even clearer if we adjust our understanding of happiness to mean growing into what we were intended to be. When we accept this definition, we will see that the quest for happiness and the quest for virtue are closely aligned.

The problem is that though everyone wants to be happy, few want to improve in virtue. I have already laid out the reason for this: because it is difficult to overcome resistance. The human heart longs for lasting joy but most seek it on terms that are impossible. Happiness is only attainable on happiness's terms. Those terms are that we must overcome resistance and develop our virtue.

Many people simply refuse to accept those terms. They spend their lives looking for some other way, some other means of achieving happiness than through the development of their character. When their attempts to find some other means fail again and again, they grow resentful, preferring to waste their vital energy on denying the truth rather than spend it in accordance with Reality.

This hostility is not always overt. It may not seem destructive. But it always stems from an underlying refusal to begin moving toward the only fulfillment that is consistently possible, the fulfillment of our character. This naturally leads to unhappiness. An unwillingness to accept happiness' terms gets nowhere because happiness does not negotiate. It's all or nothing with happiness.

This does not mean that there is no such thing as growing in happiness. There is. While we must each say a final yes or no to reality, the moments of our day-to-day lives are less binary. In most of our lives we come to grips with the demands of reality slowly, accustoming ourselves a little at a time to truths we might find hard to accept. In this way, we mature. Just as an apple tree does not pop forth from the ground laden with fruit, so we grow into our acceptance of reality.

To do this means navigating out from self-centeredness toward humility. We all begin life imagining that we are at the center of reality. This is an inherent part of childhood. When we are very small, our needs are so great that we assume the world exists only to meet them. We cry and someone magically appears to feed or comfort us. The world appears to cater to our self-centeredness for a while.

If we are lucky enough to be around people equipped to lead us out of our self-centeredness, we will grow up. As we mature, we will grow in confidence, in our ability to meet our own needs. We will come to see that we have a place in the world and that place is not in the center of it. The love of our family and community buffers our ego against this blow, and we settle into our newfound place in life ready to accept it and to become content.

This transition rarely happens as smoothly as I have described. Instead of making a smooth transition from the self-centeredness of infancy to the settled fulfillment of adulthood, most of us hit some kind of snag or roadblock. We experience trauma. We suffer serious losses. Something happens that throws our path of growth off course and we spend years wandering, trying to get back on the right road.

Some never find the road again. People stuck wandering retain the illusion that they can dictate what reality is or, at least, what it ought to be. People are slow to give up this illusion for several reasons. One is that maintaining an illusion of power buffers their feelings of vulnerability in difficult situations.

Virtue and Happiness

Virtue Means Surrendering to Reality

People who have been traumatized sometimes lose the ability to feel safe. They may experience an ongoing tension so subtle that they become accustomed to it. They may even cease to be conscious of it. This tension can easily flare up into full-blown panic when something reminds them of the original situation or elicits the intense feelings which the original trauma engendered.

A sense that we somehow hold the power to determine how reality can or should be can be a comfort, even if an illusory one. It's no wonder people struggling with trauma can be hesitant to surrender such a belief. The problem is that refusing to relinquish our demands and expectations for reality leads not to greater happiness but to less.

Additionally, people who have been traumatized have, by definition, all experienced some sort of boundary violation. Someone crossed a line or violated their will in a hurtful, often devastating way. When we experience these kinds of intense boundary violations, we can go through life with an unusually high sense of vulnerability.

The more vulnerable we feel, the more difficult surrendering to reality can seem. Even trying to lower our defenses may make us feel more vulnerable. This strategy necessarily backfires as our defenses separate us from others, cause friction in our relationships, harm our physical health, and cause us to perceive others and their motives in a skewed way. The result, of course, is more unhappiness.

The only fully healthy and rewarding course of action for those who have been traumatized is the same as the only fully healthy and rewarding course of action for us all. We must move away from our self-centered defensiveness and accept the conditions of happiness which means to accept reality.

Reality insists we drop our demands, and surrender our fantasies about what life ought to be. We must instead accept what is. Approaching reality open-handed, not clinging to our expectations, resentments and agendas, is the beginning of happiness. This is what it means to accept happiness' terms: that we come without demands and instead cultivate not not merely acceptance but affection for what is.

This does not mean we stop wanting things. We can still have goals and dreams, but we cease to see the fulfillment of these desires as the ground of happiness and instead see that their fulfillment stems from our acceptance and love for what is. People who see the fulfillment of their hopes and dreams as the necessary ground for happiness end up very stressed.

Demanding that our goals be achieved before we allow ourselves to be happy fills us with anxiety and a constant sense of pressure. Better to know what we would like to achieve, but not to make our happiness dependent on those things.

When we are willing to drop our agendas and simply love what is, we come into full contact with the real. The strangeness and mystery of our existence, even as it is expressed through simple things like the beauty of a flower or the sound of frogs in the night, can penetrate our hearts. When that happens, we can see all our demands and agendas and defense mechanisms were actually preventing us from experiencing the peace we longed for. This is the goal of all our growth: to become the kind of person who can enter into life and its wonder without defense.

Dropping our Defenses

This does not mean we must make ourselves foolishly vulnerable. To encounter reality with fewer defenses doesn't mean we have to ignore the dangers present in the world. It simply means that we live in the world with a realistic assessment of danger, that we do not allow past traumas to cause us to imagine the dangers are greater than they are nor do we allow our need for comfort and distraction to drive us into recklessness.

Knowing we can deal with threats as they arise rather than always anticipating them allows us to lower our defenses. Relaxing our defenses then leads to a freedom that is part of our happiness. It is toward this freedom that our actions and choices should aim.

Unhappy people are not free. Their defenses hem them in. They are bound by the chains of vice and refusal of responsibility. The unhappy blame their unhappiness on their bad experiences. They imagine their unhappiness is an inevitable result of the poor treatment they received or of some other set of negative circumstances.

It's easy to see why. Many people go through extremely difficult and painful circumstances. These people deserve empathy. We should do all we can to help people who have suffered to recover and make the most of their lives. The first step in doing that is to encourage them to take full responsibility for their decisions and for the future those choices bring into being. The first step toward helping them drop their defenses is to encourage them to take responsibility and to grow in virtue.

Virtue and Happiness

It can be hard for people who have suffered to accept that they must take responsibility for their lives. Too often suffering can engender a hurdle in the quest for happiness many cannot get over. When people refuse to take responsibility for their lives, they nurture a distorted view of reality. They reinforce defenses that keep them at odds with what is and that condone their vices. All of these are the opposite of what happiness requires.

Suffering people can misunderstand the necessity of taking responsibility in two equally tragic ways. An encouragement to assume full responsibility for our lives can be misunderstood as saying we are responsible for the damaging things others did to us. Second, it can be misunderstood as a way of saying that what was done to us was not that bad. Both are wrong.

Suffering, the Impediment to Responsibility

The first is wrong because just as we are responsible for all of our thoughts, words, feelings, decisions and actions, so others are for theirs. When others choose to behave in ways that damage us, the responsibility for that behavior does not shift to us, though those who abused us may try to convince us otherwise.

Too often, people who have been mistreated assume they are in some way to blame for that mistreatment, and may suffer years of negative feelings as a result. Far from reducing the importance of keeping the lines of responsibility straight, this fact emphasizes how important it is to clarify these lines. When we own our thoughts, feelings, words, choices and actions, remaining clear on what we are responsible for and what we are not becomes easier. Nothing insulates us against the pressure to assume blame for other people's bad behavior like a willingness to assume responsibility for our own.

The one caveat to this is that there are situations where people are victimized in such a way as to make their own responsibility in a situation negligible. Crime victims fit into this category, for example. We cannot say that a man who is mugged deserved it because he was in a known high-crime area. The people who made the area high-crime in the first place can never transfer their responsibility to their victim under any circumstances. A man mugged in a high-crime area has done nothing wrong by exercising his freedom to be there and in no way does his behavior condone or justify his victimization.

However, even crime victims remain in the same situation with respect to responsibility as everyone else. They are responsible for facing what has happened to them and taking responsibility for making the most of their lives and characters. That may seem unfair. It may seem that severe victimization should excuse one from the burdens of virtue and success. But it does not.

Nor is this reality unfair. It is not unfair because everyone is under the same burden. Everyone must take responsibility. Everyone must shoulder the burden of his developing character. Everyone must be responsible for the quality of his life. No one is singled out, no one excepted. How can a reality so universal, so complete be unfair?

Having to accept responsibility for our lives does not mean that the things we have suffered are somehow not that bad. Many people seem to have an unconscious assumption that healing from trauma, which is just another way of taking responsibility for ourselves, indicates that what happened to us was not as terrible as it seemed. Sometimes people are reluctant to take responsibility to heal because they believe healing shows that what they suffered was not devastating. That is not true. Healing does not prove that trauma was not devastating, but that the spirit within was stronger even than the offense.

The Importance of Assuming Responsibility

Why spend all this time on the importance of taking responsibility? Because taking responsibility is at the core of developing virtue, and developing virtue is at the core of becoming happy. Happy people focus on what they can do, on whether their behavior is virtuous. Unhappy people blame others.

Refusing to take responsibility for the development of our characters is a strategy for avoiding pain. We hope that if we refuse to take the responsibility, someone else will agree to take the pain. We know intuitively that the pursuit of virtue will cause pain. We will have to exert effort. We will have to confront scary things. We could get hurt.

The Pursuit of Virtue Hurts

Just as Edmund in C.S. Lewis's "The Voyage of the Dawn Treader" must, when he has been transformed into a dragon, submit to the painful process of Aslan's splitting and tearing away the dragon skin so the real boy can

Virtue and Happiness

emerge,[1] so too must we submit to the painful process of growth if we are to be what we could. Yes, the process of pursuing virtue, of transforming our character sometimes hurts.

If we are to proceed down this line, we must accept two obvious facts. First, we must accept that there is no real, lasting avoidance of pain, and second, we must accept that not all pain is bad. We must learn to distinguish the good pain from the bad. The end result of all our attempts to avoid pain is greater and unnecessary pain.

This is obvious when we consider something as simple as exercise. The man who takes up jogging must suffer. He must endure the jarring of his muscles when his feet hit the concrete, he must suffer the burning of his lungs as their capacity is enhanced. He must suffer the embarrassment of the neighbors seeing his first awkward movements as he goes flailing down the sidewalk. He can choose this pain. Should he want to avoid this short-term pain and forego his exercise routine, he will only be postponing, not eliminating the pain from his life. The pain will come back later in worse and more punishing forms.

We all know this. We know that small pains must be taken now to avoid great pains later. This is an ironclad law of reality. We do not break it when we ignore it. We break only ourselves. The call to develop our virtue and to escape our vices is the call to pay the smaller bill now.

When we do choose to pay the smaller bill now, it does not take long to learn to distinguish between the kinds of pain we experience. Stick with it long enough, and you will notice that the right kind of pain is always accompanied by its companion: joy. The bad kind of pain merely brings despair. The guy who comes home from his first run will be full of endorphins and a sense of accomplishment. The guy who sits home on the couch day after day will be full of hopelessness and self-loathing. The choice, when you break it down, is obvious.

The truth is that only by committing to a journey of developing our character can we become what we are supposed to be. Only by enduring whatever amount of good pain is required can we, like Edmund, cease to be the dragon and be freed to be the highest version of ourselves. There is no transformation without pain, and so to choose a transforming journey of character development is to choose pain.

---

1. Lewis, *The Voyage of the Dawn Treader*, 109

Given that pain is, well, painful, the question of why we ought not try to avoid it as much as possible arises. Why not simply live dependent on the comforts and escapes available and avoid suffering where it can be avoided?

The answer is joy. The answer is that as we accept the pain involved in the improvement of our character, we dig within ourselves an invisible reservoir. The amount of joy we are able to hold increases. For this reason, the beginning of our journey is always the worst part. At that point, we may find that our first steps in the right direction are the hardest, like the man going out for his first morning run. Our inner reservoir of joy is also smallest at the beginning. And so, when we begin any new journey toward wholeness, integration and virtue, we find that we must take the hardest steps at a time when our capacity for receiving inner rewards is the smallest.

This is particularly true if we have been waylaid. In an ideal situation, people learn these truths as children, taught by parents who themselves have pursued their own character development and are able to train their children to begin overcoming resistance in those early days.

But this is not the case for everyone. Many of us must learn these lessons as adults. When we do, we are often more motivated by the promise of increased joy than by some abstract desire to possess greater virtue. That is as it should be. The desire to experience joy does not mean we are selfish. Even Jesus, we are told, endured the cross "for the joy set before him."[2] The desire for joy can motivate great and noble acts and should therefore not be shunned.

The point of virtue is not to end our life with a moral high score as if life were a video game. The point of pursuing virtue is joy. Because joy alone is the destiny of the human being. For joy, we were made. For joy, we endure the pain of growth.

And so, the pursuit of virtue, in the end is the pursuit of joy. We must not shrink from this quest because to do so is to condemn ourselves to lives of dissatisfaction and bitterness, lives in which the glory inside each of us remains hidden, covered by the grime of selfishness, of trauma, of fear and of misery. The pursuit of virtue and the shunning of vice is the process of uncovering that glory which radiates only joy. This is why we are here. We must delay no longer. The road to joy lies always before us. Let us go now and walk it together.

---

2. Hebrews 12: 2 (ESV).

Bibliography

Aristotle. *Nichomachean Ethics.* Oxford: Oxford University Press, 1980.

Berry, Wendell. "A Half Pint of Old Darling." Story of the Week (The Library of America), accessed February 25, 2021, https://loa-shared.s3.amazonaws.com/static/pdf/Berry_Half-Pint.pdf.

Covey, Stephen. *The Seven Habits of Highly Effective People.* New York: Simon & Schuster, 1989.

———. *The Seven Habits of Highly Effective People.* New York: Simon and Schuster, 1989.

Eliot, George. *Silas Marner.* New York: Barnes & Noble, 1996.

Frankl, Viktor. *Man's Search for Meaning.* Boston: Beacon, 1992.

Hayden, Erik. "Study Says College Says College Students Don't Learn Very Much." *The Atlantic,* January 18, 2011. https://www.theatlantic.com/culture/archive/2011/01/study-says-college-students-don-t-learn-very-much/342624/.

John, Tara. "How the World's First Loneliness Minister Will Tackle 'the Sad Reality of Modern Life.'" *TIME,* April 25, 2018. https://time.com/5248016/tracey-crouch-uk-loneliness-minister/.

Junod, Tom. "Can You Say . . . Hero?" The Neighborhood Archive. Accessed February 25, 2021. http://www.neighborhoodarchive.com/publications/press/esquire/index.html.

Lewis, C. S. *The Voyage of the Dawn Treader.* New York: Harper Collins, 1952.

Pressfield, Stephen. *The War of Art.* Black Irish Entertainment LLC, 2002.

Sommerville, John. *How the News Makes Us Dumb.* Downers Grove: InterVarsity, 1999.

Thompson, Flora. *Lark Rise to Candleford: A Trilogy.* Penguin, 1973.

White, Marian. "US Moving Statistics for 2019." October 24, 2019. https://www.moving.com/tips/us-moving-statistics-for-2019/.

www.ingramcontent.com/pod-product-compliance
Lightning Source LLC
Chambersburg PA
CBHW051930160426
43198CB00012B/2090